Praise for *The First Years Matter: Becoming an Effective Teacher*

"Carol Pelletier Radford is the consummate professional educator. From the outset of my association with her, she has been a conscientious and dedicated administrator, a mentor, and a generous and supportive colleague. Readily able to foster constructive connections between course material and her own exemplary classroom experience, she has consistently provided innovative direction and support to classroom teachers by way of the books she has authored. Generations of educators have and will continue to use them.

Dr. Radford's commitment to teaching in urban populations has distinguished her contribution to the education profession. I continue to be impressed by her command of relevant research and effective instructional techniques. Her skill is facilitating communication. She effectively addresses the interface between practice and education with the primary objective of identifying the relevant issues in support of human well-being. Dr. Radford is truly a reflective practitioner, and I always appreciate opportunities to learn from her as she continues to clarify the relevant issues in educational practice by way of her latest publications."

—Cameron Marzelli, Adjunct Faculty at the Graduate School of Arts and Social Sciences, Lesley University; Founder, stillwoman.com: Using the Expressive Arts on the Resilience Path

"What amazes me about the Mentoring in Action *and* The First Years Matter *books is that every aspect of the teaching field is addressed."*

—Kerri Schoonover, History Teacher
Atlantis Charter High School

"I love the idea of having mentors and mentees work alongside each other with Mentoring in Action *and* The First Years Matter, *sharing their thoughts about challenges and successes each month and opening up a reflective dialogue."*

—Karen Mayotte, Grade 2 Classroom Teacher / Co-coordinator Mentor Program
Nashoba Regional School District

"The two texts, Mentoring in Action *and* The First Years Matter, *are companion texts that give both participants a guide for discussions, suggestions for activities, and a place to track reflections. They also allow for targeted differentiation."*

—Maureen Perkins, Reading Specialist
William A. Berkowitz School

"Integrating teacher evaluation standards fits naturally into the reflection prompts and activities in The First Years Matter *and* Mentoring in Action *texts."*

—Caitlin Corrieri, Mentor Coordinator
Belmont Public Schools

"I will most definitely use the Mentoring in Action *text paired with* The First Years Matter *text as a month-by-month curriculum to focus mentoring conversations."*

—Kristen Daly, First Grade Teacher
Kenneth Coombs School

"With the Mentoring in Action *and* The First Years Matter *books, training of mentors is consistent and comprehensive. The First Years Matter is structured enough to provide a clear path toward helping a new hire to achieve independence."*

—John Radosta, Mentoring Coordinator
Milton High School

The First Years Matter: Becoming an Effective Teacher

A Mentoring Guide for Novice Teachers

Second Edition

Carol Pelletier Radford

Foreword by Peter DeWitt

CORWIN

A SAGE Publishing Company

FOR INFORMATION:

Corwin
A SAGE Company
2455 Teller Road
Thousand Oaks, California 91320
(800) 233-9936
www.corwin.com

SAGE Publications Ltd.
1 Oliver's Yard
55 City Road
London, EC1Y 1SP
United Kingdom

SAGE Publications India Pvt. Ltd.
B 1/I 1 Mohan Cooperative Industrial Area
Mathura Road, New Delhi 110 044
India

SAGE Publications Asia-Pacific Pte. Ltd.
3 Church Street
#10-04 Samsung Hub
Singapore 049483

Acquisitions Editor: Ariel Bartlett
Senior Associate Editor: Desirée A. Bartlett
Senior Editorial Assistant: Andrew Olson
Production Editor: Veronica Stapleton
                                       Hooper
Copy Editor: Beth Hammond
Typesetter: C&M Digitals (P) Ltd.
Proofreader: Alison Syring
Indexer: Jeanne Busemeyer
Cover Designer: Gail Buschman
Marketing Manager: Jill Margulies

This book was previously published by: Pearson Education, Inc.

Printed in the United States of America.

Library of Congress Cataloging-in-Publication Data

Names: Radford, Carol Pelletier, author.

Title: The first years matter : becoming an effective teacher : a mentoring guide for novice teachers / Carol Pelletier Radford.

Description: Second edition. | Thousand Oaks, California : Corwin, A SAGE Company, [2016] | Includes index.

Identifiers: LCCN 2016011755 | ISBN 9781506345062 (pbk. : alk. paper)

Subjects: LCSH: Mentoring in education—Handbooks, manuals, etc. | First year teachers—Supervision of—Handbooks, manuals, etc.

Classification: LCC LB1731.4 .R32 2016 | DDC 371.102—dc23

LC record available at https://lccn.loc.gov/2016011755

This book is printed on acid-free paper.

19 20 10 9 8 7 6 5

CONTENTS

AUGUST

SEPTEMBER

BEGINNING THE SCHOOL YEAR SUCCESSFULLY:
Creating a Community of Learners in the Classroom

OCTOBER

NOVEMBER

DECEMBER

JANUARY

FEBRUARY

MARCH

APRIL

MAY

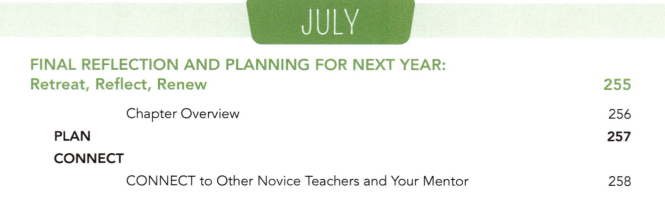

JUNE

JULY

ACT

REFLECT

SET GOALS   **262**

Note from the Publisher: The author has provided video and web content throughout the book which is available to you through QR Codes. To read a QR Code, you must have a smartphone or tablet with a camera. We recommend that you download a QR Code reader app that is made specifically for your phone or tablet brand.

FOREWORD

Do you remember when you first became a teacher? I will never forget my first full year with "*my own*" class. As a novice teacher in a city school district, I couldn't wait to see my students make their way into the classroom. I had these pre-conceived notions that I could close the door and just be with the students. I felt that by the time they were done learning from me that they would be reading Moby Dick. Perhaps even more than reading a great novel, they would be able to dig deeper like in the movie Dead Poet's Society, one by one students would stand up on their tables reciting one of the great works that they would have read with me over a period of months. Sure, I was teaching first grade, but they would certainly show amazing growth in their learning. After all, I was a novice teacher with a great deal of freshly learned instructional knowledge under my belt.

The excitement to know that all of my hard work in college was paying off and I was now a real life teacher was sometimes overwhelming. And that was before the year ever began. All the planning that we do as novice teachers, although important, may have to be thrown away as soon as the students enter the classroom because they bring experiences we can't always plan for. Like those of you who taught for the first time, I soon realized I was working without a net. I was no longer a student teacher or a teaching assistant. I was responsible for the 30 first graders that couldn't sit still for two minutes in front of me. That was where the fun and the fear all began.

There were nights I laid awake worried about what they went home to, and had countless students, like all of you, who hugged me at the end of the day and didn't want to go home. After my first year was completed, I remember standing in the classroom all alone wondering what happened. I was supposed to be the one teaching them, but I learned as much from them as they did from me.

Over the years I learned that teaching was not an individual sport, but one that took collaboration. Whether it was working as a grade level team, or with the special education teacher because I taught inclusionary education, I soon realized that teaching was a lifelong learning experience, which made me love it even more. And the learning didn't stop there. I learned form the parents who came to the parent-teacher conferences with baggage from when they were students, and I learned from the parents who were a bit older and wiser than me, who wanted nothing more than the best experience for their children.

I always remember my first years with great fondness, and those years had an enormous impact on my first years as a school leader. The first year teachers that we are fortunate enough to hire are the ones that we have to devote extra energy to get to know. Many of us sit on interview committees, find the best candidates, hire them, and then walk away. We say we will check in with them. We say we will give them some of our resources and an undivided attention where we sit down with them to go through those resources that will be most helpful. And then life happens, and each of those days that we promised to make an effort get filled with our own distraction and focuses.

And that is why I love *The First Years Matter: Becoming An Effective Teacher*. Our first year of teaching is really complicated, but it seems to be even more complicated these days in comparison to when I was a novice teacher, and Radford understands that. With accountability, mandates, district initiatives, and testing, teaching is not for the faint-hearted, and Carol Radford understands that as well.

Carol Radford brilliantly lays out all of those things we need to know and how to get through them. In leadership circles we talk a lot about "*We don't know what we don't know*" and our "*Blind spots.*" What is great about this book is that Carol clues us all into what we should know, and how to get through it, so that we are less likely to have as many blind spots. She lays out a perfectly executed action plan which includes creating a community of learners, the mentoring process, and understanding our impact as teachers. These are all issues that we need to know about, not just in our first years, but every year we teach and lead. Radford closes out each section with her Plan, Connect and Act, which helps novice teachers, and their leaders, prepare for each day.

Our first years as teachers were exciting, difficult and scary. I would never take my struggles as a novice teacher away, but I certainly wish I had this book to help me better prepare for them.

Peter M. DeWitt, EdD
Corwin Author/Consultant
Finding Common Ground *Blog (Education Week).*

PREFACE

This second edition of *The First Years Matter* brings a new title that includes an important message. By adding an *s* to years, we are noting that the first *years* matter to novice teachers. Teaching is an ongoing learning process; you can't learn how to teach in one year! As a beginner, it is important to realize that the first *few years* are developmental. Throughout the book, we will be referring to teachers in their second year and beyond as "2+ year teachers." Novice teachers in their second, third, and even fourth years of teaching have shared that using the book for another year is useful because they now know what to expect and this book reminds them of effective teaching practices. So don't try to do all the activities this year. Save the book and use it next year too!

Your mentor is using the *Mentoring in Action* book that is aligned to this one so that you have a common language for your mentoring meetings. By having your own book, you will be empowered to look ahead at topics for all the months, skip around and read what is most meaningful to you, and bring your own questions to meetings. Watch Video 0.1, *Using the First Year Matters: Being Mentored in Action*, to hear novice teachers talk about having their own book. Go to the Companion Website or scan the QR code on a mobile device.

VIDEO 0.1

Using the First Year Matters: Being Mentored in Action

The second edition of *The First Years Matter* introduces new tools and topics to expand your strategies for becoming an effective teacher. The new cover image of the tree branches reaching out illustrates your growth over time. A Novice Teacher Affirmation on every month's chapter title page places an emphasis on mindfulness and intentional teaching. This edition also encourages you to align your mentoring conversations with your own state or district teacher evaluation standards. Listening to students is integrated throughout this book to emphasize the importance of their voices in your development as an effective teacher. So whether you are stepping into the classroom for the first time or continuing your mentoring experience as a 2+ year teacher, I hope you will find this resource practical and inspiring.

The second edition includes these features:

- Twelve month curriculum with the addition of July for reflecting and planning
- Cues for 2+ year teachers to *go further* into a strategy or reflection
- Parts I and II revised and updated to include novice teacher leadership ideas
- Chapter overviews with updated InTASC standards and video introductions
- PLAN pages now updated to include strategies for collaborating with your mentor using observation
- Updated CONNECT pages that include Hot Topics and ways to include Student Voices
- ACT pages that list key questions and a First ACT page aligned to standards
- The REFLECT section with new Mindful Teaching Dilemmas
- SET GOALS pages with a focus on your social and emotional development
- A QR Code within book chapters to access videos on mobile devices
- The Companion Website, which includes the videos and digital forms indicated in the chapters
- A Novice Teacher Journal to record your thoughts and ideas throughout the year also available on the Companion Website

ACKNOWLEDGMENTS

A profound and emotional shift came to me on the day I interviewed a high school student named Jennifer Rossado. She was a student in Jim Strader's classroom who had improved her math grade from an F to an A. Jim Strader was a graduate of a teacher preparation program that I led at the university, and he was also mentoring a novice teacher. I wanted to know about this success story, so I could pass his secret on to other beginning teachers.

Jennifer agreed to be recorded with only me in the room with the videographer. She was visibly nervous and not forthcoming in the beginning of the interview. She shared she was doing this only because Mr. Strader was the best teacher she had ever had and he made a difference in her life.

I thank Jennifer for her honesty and courage to speak up that day and be recorded knowing this would be shared with others. She spoke from her heart with her knees shaking and her voice cracking. She told me that Mr. Strader didn't judge her or give up on her. Jim Strader taught Jennifer how to do math, so she could feel successful in school and have a future.

VIDEO 0.2

Teachers Make a Difference

Matt Conley and I sat in the basement of an old high school listening to this vulnerable student share what it meant to have a teacher who could help her achieve in school. Thank you, Matt, for editing a two-hour session to a three-minute clip that captured Jennifer's message. Video 0.2, *Teachers Make a Difference*, is the very first video I ever produced. Jennifer's courage to speak up inspired me to continue to use video as a way to communicate to teachers in my courses.

Shonna McGrail Ryan and Adam Pelletier continued producing and editing the videos that you will see referenced in this book. Shonna's ability to design courses that integrated video allowed me to transition to teaching online. Adam's tireless editing and ability to capture the true message in a video demonstrates his creative talent. Thank you both for being on this journey with me. You make this book come alive with the voices of students, teachers, mentors, and coaches.

To learn the secret of Jim Strader's success with Jennifer, watch Matt Conley's video, *Teachers Make a Difference* on the companion website or by using the quick response (QR) code. All other videos produced by Shonna and Adam are available on MentoringinAction.com.

ABOUT THE AUTHOR

Carol Pelletier Radford is an education consultant recently transitioning from the position of Project SUCCESS Program Director, a Massachusetts statewide hybrid mentor "train the trainer" leadership program. She received her EdD from Harvard University where she focused her studies on teacher leadership, preparing cooperating teachers, and professional development. She has served in higher education for 20 years working as an administrator, a licensing officer, and alternative certification program director.

In more than 20 years as a public school teacher, she has received numerous teacher leadership awards, among them the prestigious Christa McAuliffe Fellowship sponsored by the U.S. Department of Education.

She is the author of *Mentoring in Action: Guiding, Sharing, and Reflecting With Novice Teachers; The First Years Matter: Becoming an Effective Teacher; Strategies for Successful Student Teaching 3rd edition; The First Year Matters: Being Mentored in Action; Mentoring in Action: A Month-By-Month Curriculum; Touch the Future TEACH!;* and *Techniques and Strategies for Coaching Student Teachers 2nd edition.*

Carol is actively engaged in using video to teach and communicate with mentors and novice teachers. Her online graduate courses include Becoming a Qualified Mentor, Maintaining Your Balance—Novice Teacher Development After Year 1, and Mindful Leadership in Action—Supporting Principals to Lead Induction Programs. She is a passionate advocate for teacher leadership and the inclusion of student voices in classroom practice. Her current focus is integrating mindfulness practices into her courses and presentations. You can find her resources and books on MentoringinAction.com.

This book is dedicated to Jim Strader, a generous human being and skillful math teacher, who passed too soon.

INTRODUCTION

WELCOME TO
THE FIRST YEARS MATTER!

If you are reading this, you are a first-year teacher beginning your career or a 2+ year teacher in a follow-up mentoring program to further develop your teaching skills. Let me begin by saying, thank you for choosing to be a teacher. You have made a commitment to students and their success in school.

As a teacher, you are responsible for your students' instruction as well as their social and emotional development. Whether you are teaching a content area or a special subject you must engage students. You are not just teaching a subject or a skill; you are interacting with human beings to help them learn and be successful in life—a big job! By putting students at the heart of your teaching you are intentionally creating a community of learners where everyone is respected. In this book, you will be encouraged to use mindfulness as a way to stay focused on your goal of being an effective teacher.

Mindfulness *noun* mind·ful·ness \ˈmīn(d)-fəl-nəs\

1. the quality or state of being mindful

2. the practice of maintaining a nonjudgmental state of heightened or complete awareness of one's thoughts, emotions, or experiences on a moment-to-moment basis; *also:* such a state of awareness

By being mindful and paying attention to what you are doing, you can purposefully apply what you are learning with your mentor, so you can help your students succeed. An important key to mindfulness is nonjudgment. Don't blame yourself for not knowing what to do. You are "learning" how to teach and choosing what works best for you in your classroom. To make those choices, you need to pay attention to your emotions and thoughts, so you can put your best ideas forward.

The goal of this book is to offer you a monthly structure, many strategies to try in your classroom, and end-of-month reflections to deepen your practice. You will be learning so many things at once, and it may get overwhelming at times. This book, along with the Novice Teacher Journal on the companion website, provides you with a place to mindfully reflect on what you are doing so you can help your students succeed in school.

Are You Prepared to Teach?

Some teachers enter teaching through traditional pathways in formal teacher preparation programs and others enroll in an alternative fast-track route. Think about the route you took and if it prepared you for the challenges of the classroom. Ask your mentor to differentiate your mentoring based on your needs. If you didn't complete a formal student teaching program, you can read this entire book and see what the year is all about. Then, as you review month-by-month, you won't be surprised by the expectations teaching brings.

I have a passion for this work. I have been a teacher and a teacher educator for more than forty years. During my visits to schools, my talks with novice teachers led me to create this second edition. My intention is to offer you an updated resource that supports you in being the most effective teacher you can be.

Enjoy your year!

Carol Pelletier Radford, EdD
MentoringinAction.com

PART I

BEGINNING YOUR JOURNEY INTO TEACHING

The Purpose of Induction and Mentoring

Mentoring is required in most states and districts to support the induction of novice teachers into the teaching profession. These programs vary, and funding is often inconsistent, so you need to find out if you are part of a formal induction program. You also need to know if your induction program has specific requirements related to your state teaching license. Ask your mentor or district administrator what you must do to meet those requirements.

If you are reading this book, you have been assigned a mentor who will guide you through your first year of teaching; or perhaps you have completed your induction year with a mentor, and you want to learn more about being an effective teacher. Your state may encourage mentoring beyond year one, and this book and the Novice Teacher Journal can provide you with a framework for meeting that requirement. Being a 2+ year teacher gives you the advantage of knowing what that first year is all about. Now you can really focus on teaching skills. In either case, it is important to understand the purposes of induction and mentoring.

The tree in Figure 1 is a visual image illustrating three purposes for mentoring. The three branches highlight topics that are important to retaining novice teachers like you in a teaching position. The roots of the mentoring and induction program are the teacher leaders in the district who serve as mentors for novice teachers like you.

Figure 1   Mentoring Program Sustainability Tree

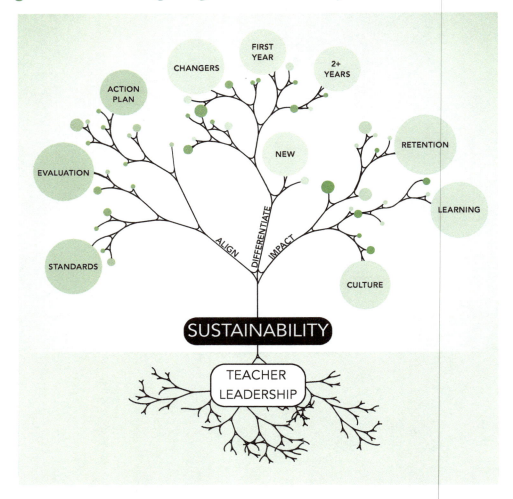

These teachers, in most cases, volunteer their time and expertise to guide you in learning how to teach and how to systematically reflect on your teaching practices.

Sustainable Mentoring

Align Mentoring Conversations to Standards

The first branch of the sustainability tree is to align your conversations and reflections to standards, teacher evaluation, and a district action plan. The Interstate Teacher Assessment and Support Consortium (InTASC) published Model Core Teaching Standards to serve as a national model. Refer to Figure 2 to review these ten standards and use them as a reference to measure your teaching skills and disposition for teaching. Each chapter will review the standards that relate to the topic featured that month.

You will be assessed and observed by your principal or department chair some time this year to determine your effectiveness in the classroom and whether you will be rehired. Review the school evaluation rubric and standards in your district to understand the criteria on which you will be measured. Some novice teachers have shared with me, "I don't have time

Figure 2 InTASC Model Core Teaching Standards

Standard	Description
1	**Learner Development** The teacher understands how learners grow and develop, recognizing that patterns of learning and development vary individually within and across the cognitive, linguistic, social, emotional, and physical areas, and designs and implements developmentally appropriate and challenging learning experiences.
2	**Learning Differences** The teacher uses understanding of individual differences and diverse cultures and communities to ensure inclusive learning environments that enable each learner to meet high standards.
3	**Learning Environments** The teacher works with others to create environments that support individual and collaborative learning, and that encourage positive social interaction, active engagement in learning, and self motivation.
4	**Content Knowledge** The teacher understands the central concepts, tools of inquiry, and structures of the discipline(s) he or she teaches and creates learning experiences that make these aspects of the discipline accessible and meaningful for learners to ensure mastery of the content.
5	**Application of Content** The teacher understands how to connect concepts and use differing perspectives to engage learners in critical thinking, creativity, and collaborative problem solving related to authentic local and global issues.
6	**Assessment** The teacher understands and uses multiple methods of assessment to engage learners in their own growth, to monitor learner progress, and to guide the teacher's and learner's decision making.
7	**Planning for Instruction** The teacher plans instruction that supports every student in meeting rigorous learning goals by drawing upon knowledge of content areas, curriculum, cross-disciplinary skills, and pedagogy, as well as knowledge of learners and the community context.
8	**Instructional Strategies** The teacher understands and uses a variety of instructional strategies to encourage learners to develop deep understanding of content areas and their connections, and to build skills to apply knowledge in meaningful ways.
9	**Professional Learning and Ethical Practice** The teacher engages in ongoing professional learning and uses evidence to continually evaluate his/her practice, particularly the effects of his/her choices and actions on others (learners, families, other professionals, and the community), and adapts practice to meet the needs of each learner.
10	**Leadership and Collaboration** The teacher seeks appropriate leadership roles and opportunities to take responsibility for student learning, to collaborate with learners, families, colleagues, other school professionals, and community members to ensure learner growth, and to advance the profession.

Developed by CCSSO's Interstate Teacher Assessment and Support Consortium (InTASC) April 2011

for mentoring because I have to focus on my teacher evaluation!" Mentoring is not an "add on" conversation. It should *be* the conversation that helps you to succeed on your teacher evaluation and license requirements.

See Figure 3 for a sample of how you can align this book to your state evaluation standards. By talking about these standards in The First ACT section each month, you will learn what they mean, and they will become second nature to you. Understanding and applying the evaluation standards in your district is important to your rehiring. Take the time to color-code this book so that you know which standards you are talking about or reading about.

Figure 3   Evaluation Alignment Tool

Directions: Each state or district has criteria for teacher evaluation. Align this book with your district evaluation process by comparing your evaluation criteria and standards with the ACTs listed each month.

Step 1. Find the rubric or district evaluation criteria headings that will be used to assess your development as a teacher. For example: Here are four standards used in one state that are used in district teacher evaluations.

1. Curriculum Planning and Assessment—This standard includes indicators such as subject matter knowledge; standards-based lessons and units, using a variety of assessments, modifications and adjustments to lessons as needed; analysis and conclusions; as well as sharing assessment results with parents and students.

2. Teaching All Students—This standard includes student engagement, quality of effort and work, diverse needs of students being met, collaborative and safe learning environment, respect for differences, as well as clear, high expectations for all students.

3. Family and Community Engagement—This standard includes a process for communicating with families, as well as culturally proficient communication options for parents and guardians.

4. Professional Culture—This standard includes reflective practice, professional learning and growth, professional collaboration with colleagues, and reliability and responsibility as a teacher.

As you read the indicators, you get a sense of what that standard means. As you read the ACTs in the Table of Contents, you can actually match each ACT topic to a standard.

Step 2: Select a color for each standard your district uses. In this sample, we use four colors, one for each standard. Pink for Curriculum, blue for Teaching all Students, green for Family and Community Engagement, and yellow for Professional Culture. You need to be familiar with the indicators listed under each standard. For example, "reflection" is listed under Professional Culture in this state so anything with "reflection" would be color-coded yellow. These colors are often included as a package for highlighters. You can also use colored dots to place on the pages instead of the highlighter.

Step 3: Review the topics listed for each chapter and scan the ACTs for each month to make a decision about which standard relates most closely to this topic. Highlight the ACT on the page in the book so you can see which standard it relates to when you are having a mentoring conversation. A sample using these four standards, titled *Aligning Standards to Mentoring in Action*, is available on the companion website. This will give you an idea of how easy this is to do! It proves to be a very important alignment as you learn how to become an effective teacher.

Your district leaders and your mentor are responsible for aligning the program goals with a district induction plan. All the novice teachers entering your school or district should be working with a common language for teaching. Your mentor may be on the District Action Plan committee, and in the future you may consider contributing to the ideas to ensure the plan meets the needs of novice teachers.

Differentiate Mentoring to Meet Your Needs

Career changers, new to district hires, 2+ year teachers, and first time in the classroom teachers have different needs. You can customize your mentoring conversations by sharing your needs with your mentor or by simply using the pages in this book as you need them. Skim the entire book and tag the pages that are most useful. Even though the book is organized by month, you don't have to do this book in order. Mindfully select the monthly ACTivities (ACTs) list that will move your teaching skills forward. If your district offers a 2+ mentoring program, you can revisit the ACT pages that you completed last year and acknowledge your continued growth over time. Date your pages, refer back to them, and use them as evidence for teacher evaluation.

Measure the Impact of Induction

The third branch of the tree highlights three areas that illustrate the possible impact of mentoring. School culture can be impacted when a community of teacher learners is created to share and support each other. Your mentor is part of this community, and you are invited to fully participate in this community with her. Students, families, and community leaders are part of your community of learners, and how you interact with them impacts the culture of the school. The success of a school culture is often measured in the retention rate of the novice teachers. How many novice teachers stay at your school? If teachers are choosing not to come back the next year or are leaving before the end of the school year, there is usually a problem. Do you know what the school culture for novice teachers is at your school? Ultimately, the greatest impact for mentoring is that the students in your classroom are successful. You are the reason there is a mentoring program! The goal is to retain you and have you be the most effective teacher you can be, so your students can thrive in your classroom and in school. Sustaining all three branches of this tree is a goal for successful induction and mentoring programs.

What Is Mentoring in Action?

Your mentor's book is titled *Mentoring in Action* because as a mentor he is "in action" when he is mentoring you. Most mentors are teaching full-time or on a reduced teaching load if there are resources in your district to provide release time for mentors. This also means that you are "being mentored in action" because you are learning to teach while you are in the act of teaching. This works because you can apply what you are learning immediately and change your practice. Your book, along with your mentor's book, provides a road map for your conversations so that you can stay focused on teaching practices that relate to the standards.

As shown in Figure 4, the goal is to create a common language with these two resources, so together you can help students succeed in the classroom. By using the companion website with the videos and forms, you can expand your thinking and integrate more resources into your teaching. The Plan–Connect–Act–Reflect–Set Goals format in both books provides a format for each chapter that is easy to follow. This format will complement your busy teaching day and allow you both to focus.

Figure 4   Mentoring in Action

Plan-Connect-Act-Reflect-Set Goals

(Vertical axis label: Companion Website Videos and Forms)

Boxes: Meeting the needs of novice teachers → Creating a common language and plan → More effective teaching in all classrooms

Building a Relationship With Your Mentor

Research shows that the most important relationship for novice teachers is the mentor. If you are fortunate enough to have an experienced teacher assigned to you, take advantage of all she has to offer. Experience brings wisdom, and you can benefit from this. The sink or swim method of inducting a novice teacher is not helpful. Yes, you do need to learn things on your own and try and fail to test your methods, but you don't need to do that all the time. Mentors are assigned to support and guide.

Your mentor is taking on this role as an extra duty because she wants to support beginning teachers to be successful. She has opened her heart to you and is serving the district and you in this role. Get to know your mentor by completing the Relationship Profile in Figure 5 with her. As you compare and share your answers to the questions, you will learn about each other. Respect each other's perspectives. You don't have to be the same teacher as your mentor. You are a different teacher, and your job is to be the best version of you, not a clone of your mentor. See Figure 5. Relationship Profile.

One of the most important ways to build a relationship is to listen. Your mentor will provide you with feedback, offer you suggestions, and discuss important issues with you. Being open to fully listening will enable you to get the most out of this experience. This doesn't mean you have to do everything your mentor suggests. It means you respectfully listen, ask questions, and integrate what works for you in your classroom. This is a learning opportunity for you.

Find out who will be evaluating you this year. Agree that whatever you share with your mentor will not be repeated to another colleague or the person who is evaluating you. Your mentor must be a confidential colleague for you to feel safe.

Dedicate yourself to reflecting on your practice and being guided by your mentor. If you do not have an assigned mentor, or if you are a 2+ year teacher, read this book and self-mentor so you can be the best teacher you can be. Watch the videos, write in your journal, and try the ACTs in your classroom. Take your role seriously and recognize the important influence you are for your students.

Figure 5 Relationship Profile

The Relationship Profile: A Process for the Mentor and Novice Teacher

Directions: Use this template as a guide to learn about each other. Feel free to add your own columns to the table. What would you like to know about your mentor? A digital copy of this form is on the companion website.

Topics	Philosophy of Teaching	Career Stage and Age	Teaching and Learning Styles	Personality and Life Goals
Questions	*Why did we choose teaching?*	*How do our ages and teaching experience compare?*	*How do we teach and how do we like to learn?* *How do we like feedback?*	*How do we interact with others?*
Novice Teacher				
Mentor				
Similarities and Differences— What Shows Up?				
Acknowledging diverse perspectives and respecting these differences publicly promotes a trusting relationship. This is one way to build a relationship with your mentor.				

Companion Website

Figure 6 Are You Listening?

Directions: Ask yourself, "Am I really listening, or am I thinking about what I want to say next?" You need to be an active listener who can hear what your mentor is saying without judging it. Being open to suggestions and changes that you may need to make is not always easy. These statements reflect some barriers to actively listening. Read each statement and rate yourself. Are you listening?

What do you do?	Always Sometimes Never!	
Do you assume what the speaker is going to say before she finishes her statement?		
Do you finish other people's sentences?		
Are you easily distracted (by phone, e-mail, someone walking by) when in a conversation?		
Do you argue or try to strongly persuade someone to do it your way?		
Would you say you like to control the conversation?		
Do you accept feedback easily?		
Are you open to suggestions?		
Do you ask people questions?		
Do you multitask in meetings or during conversations?		
Do you put your phone on silent when you are in a meeting?		
Are you writing your shopping list in your head (or for real on paper) while listening?		

Your mentor will empower you to share your best practices to help you emerge as a novice teacher leader who will stay in the district. Don't worry about having the *perfect mentor* this year. Learn from the mentor that is assigned to you and ask questions. Don't get too focused on your personalities and social connections. Your role is to be engaged in the process, so you can discover ways to better teach your students. Listen and learn.

Social and Emotional Learning. Teaching is emotionally draining at times, and because we are all humans with lives outside of school, you will have personal issues arise during the school year. You always should let your mentor know if there is a stressful situation going on in your life. You don't have to share the details, just that there is some personal challenge you are facing. Your mentor may feel compelled to provide advice and share her own personal stories. It is best not to engage in a focus on your personal life. Keep your mentoring conversations on student learning. It may be very difficult for you, but the best advice you can get is to leave your personal issues at the door.

VIDEO 1.1

Managing Your Stress to Promote Well-Being

Developing your own social and emotional learning *is* something you can talk about with your mentor. This means that you will learn how to minimize your anxiety and promote your own well-being and health. Take some time to watch Video 1.1, *Managing Your Stress to Promote Well-Being* and Video 1.2, *Managing Your Stress: Take a Break,* available on the companion website. You may consider watching these videos with your mentor and having a mentoring conversation about this topic. Your goal is to teach your students and stay healthy and focused on the development of their social and emotional needs. You may find these videos give you some ideas to use with your students too.

The Board of Mentors process can also assist you in reflecting on who can help you with any social and emotional issues. Moving to a new town, having a parent pass away, and just getting your first full-time job are all emotional issues that could influence the way you teach students. Your mentor cannot meet all of these needs for you. His role is to guide you to proficiency on the teaching standards. Yes, you may "connect" with your mentor, but it isn't fair to have him take on all of these social and emotional needs that you may face. That is why this process will enlighten you to discover who in your life can help you. The more people sitting on your board of mentors, the more help you have to navigate your year of teaching. Use the Board of Mentors process shown in Figure 7 to find out who is sitting at your table. A digital version is available on the companion website.

VIDEO 1.2

Managing Your Stress: Take a Break

Use a mindfulness stance when you are assessing your social and emotional development. Be purposeful when you complete the Are You Listening? assessment and the Board of Mentors processes. Bring the intention of nonjudgment to yourself and others to maintain a healthy disposition toward your teaching practice. This year is about practice not being perfect. Being in the moment, aware of your emotions and feelings, will give you strength to do what is right for you. Use these tools to give you a knowledge base for developing your own social and emotional skills. Instead of discussing your *stories about your challenges* use your time to discuss the strategies available for promoting healthy reactions to any life situation.

Group Mentoring and Novice Teacher Leadership. Group mentoring is a valuable way to connect with other novice teachers in your school or district who are in their first year or 2+ years. The Group Mentoring Agenda in Figure 8 is one way to organize these meetings. Mentors often lead these meetings, but you may consider coleading if you are a 2+ year teacher who is ready for a leadership role. Sharing best practices is a great way to let everyone at the meeting talk and share. The mentor doesn't always have to even attend every meeting. She can just help you get started. An interactive portable document format (PDF) titled "Group Mentoring" is available on the companion website. This resource includes videos and examples of agendas for two types of mentoring groups. The Problems to Possibilities video is led by a mentor, and the Sharing Best Practices video is led by a novice teacher.

Figure 7   Board of Mentors Process

Directions: Use this tool in discovering who is in your support system. Your mentor is only one person and cannot meet all the social and emotional needs you may have this year. A digital version of this form is available on the companion website.

Print your name in one of the chairs at the table. Notice that YOU are the leader of your Board of Directors. There is a blank line near every chair, and the line is where you will print the "role" the person who is sitting in that chair plays in your life. Your role is to reflect on your practice and make appropriate changes as well as to acknowledge your successes. For example, your line would say reflective practitioner because your role is to reflect on your teaching practices. Your mentor's name is on a chair next to you, and that role would be mentor. Another person's role may be "best friend" or "financial advice." Everyone sitting at your table has a role, and their name is listed in the chair.

In a conversation with your mentor, or in your own personal reflection, discover the names of the people in your life who support you in different ways. For example, if you are moving to a new apartment, your best friend might be your mentor. We all have mentors who help us with finances, social networking, spiritual support, and educational decisions. Your role in this process is to list the people in your life and what role they serve. This will allow you to see that your mentor is not your entire support system, just one of many on your Board of Mentors. You are the head of the Board and make the final decisions as to who will provide you with the support you need to be successful.

Figure 8   The Group Mentoring Agenda

Directions: As a novice teacher, you may find you want and need to talk with other beginners. Watch the video *Sharing Best Practices: Emerging Teacher Leaders,* available on the companion website, to see a novice leading a group of novice teachers in sharing ideas that relate to teaching standards.

Tips for a successful group mentoring session! Find a comfortable space and put a sign on the door that says Group Mentoring Meeting in session—Do not disturb! Invite the novices to bring snacks and drinks to share. Host the first meeting in your classroom to model a meeting. Rotate meetings to other teachers' classrooms each month. Share your classroom and why you set it up the way you have it. Ask the novices to bring their *The First Years Matter* books to the meeting. Some novice teachers like to meet before school and call the meeting the breakfast club, or after school for coffee. A meeting with three or four people is a great way to start.

Sample Agenda—30 Minutes

Welcome and introductions: Novice teacher leader shares her classroom. You take a few minutes to show something in the room that you are proud of that is working well. Review *The First Years Matter* book and see if they have any questions from the PLAN section that need to be addressed this month.

Take some time to be quiet: Select a prompt from the REFLECT page this month and ask everyone to write a response. Report on the responses and discuss the issues that come up.

Share a best practice with the group: Ask everyone to share a best practice they are using in their classroom.

Mindful teaching dilemmas: (optional) Each month there is a dilemma presented in the REFLECT section of the chapter. You may consider taking some time if you have a longer meeting scheduled to explore this dilemma together using the Mindful Journaling process.

Problems to possibilities: Novice teachers may bring up challenges and problems they are facing in this meeting. Explain that this is a sharing meeting and you will bring the issue to your mentor who will advise you about how this can be resolved. It is important as the leader to stop gossip in its tracks and not use this time as a complaint session. It is easy to piggyback on problem issues; and then soon the meeting turns to a grip session about what is not working. Take the high road and keep on track with sharing ideas.

Wrapping up the discussion: If everyone doesn't share this time, then begin the meeting with that teacher next time. Take a moment to connect whatever you talked about to the teaching standards.

Closing and acknowledgment: Thank everyone for coming and end the meeting on time.

Watch the novice teacher lead the *Sharing Best Practices* meeting video and see if this is something you might like to do in the future. Sharing ideas and solving common teaching problems is effective and practical. Novice teachers don't even have to be at the same grade level or in the same content area to learn from each other. It is also fun to socialize a bit and share survival stories. Your mentor is a wonderful support system, but it is empowering to expand your board of mentors to include a novice teacher support group!

Purposeful Mentoring Conversations

Novice teachers often ask, "What are we supposed to talk about when we meet?" This book can be used for conversation starters with your mentor. If your mentor is using the *Mentoring in Action* book, he may guide the conversations to topics that are most relevant to your school or district goals. But you can also read the chapters ahead of time and come prepared to a mentoring meeting to discuss a topic that is of particular interest to you. The ACTs in each chapter provide you with many options for conversations. Use the book as a resource from which you can pick and choose the topics and pages that would be the meaningful conversations based on your needs. The questions in the PLAN section of each chapter also offer you options for conversations based on your questions.

Purposeful mentoring conversations are those that are planned and that forward teaching skills and strategies for the classroom. By reflecting on what is important and what is the next step to improve your practice, you can minimize the overwhelming details of day-to-day teaching. The First ACT in each chapter is a place for you to align your goals to the standards. This is where you will make that important connection to how you will be assessed in your district. This book will provide you with the tools and the structure. It is your role to make your mentoring conversations meaningful and customized to address your particular need or focus.

Documenting and Sharing Your Teaching. School districts assess and evaluate the success of a teacher in a variety of ways. All districts will have standards and expectations for proficiency, and these must be discussed in your mentoring conversations. Sometimes we assume novice teachers understand evaluation and standards. Clarify any questions you have now about what is expected for your district or state license.

Align the book to your state or district standards as soon as possible so that you and your mentor can discuss how the ACT topics relate to the required standards. Simply by color-coding the book to your standards, you will create a visual connection that can easily be individualized to your state or district. Use the Evaluation Alignment Tool shown in Figure 3 to guide your process.

Observation and feedback are important components of learning how to teach because they provide your mentor with evidence of success in your classroom. Some mentors don't have release time to observe their mentee in action, and often your lesson preparation times do not match. If this is the case for you, I encourage you to use video technology to have your mentor observe and provide feedback to you.

Explore the options in your district for scheduling a high school student to come to your room to record a lesson you want your mentor to see you teach. You can even get your students involved to "create" the video and introduce themselves to your mentor! Use a mobile device if video equipment is not available. You don't need a long video. A 10–20 minute clip that includes highlights of the beginning of a lesson and some activity in the middle and the closing of the lesson will give your mentor an idea of how you are presenting yourself in the classroom.

Figure 9 Developing a Portfolio

Directions: Review any requirements regarding the organization of a portfolio with your mentor. Portfolios can be shared with parents at open house night or with district administrators who are evaluating you. A portfolio brings your teaching to life and offers the reader visual representations of you in action.

Follow these steps and discuss these ideas with your mentor. A digital version of this form is available on the companion website.

1. Review the purpose of a professional portfolio with your mentor. Why is it an important tool for a novice teacher?

2. Write a three-paragraph philosophy statement. Use this as a format.

    a. List three words to describe yourself as a teacher and why these are important.

    b. Write three beliefs you have about teaching and learning.

    c. List three ways you demonstrate your words and beliefs in the classroom.

3. Collect artifact samples in a box or online folder to be reviewed later.

    a. Student work, lesson plans, photographs, evaluation comments, professional development, and courses of students working in the classroom. Remember to get permissions for any photos you put into your portfolio.

4. Discuss the best way to present your portfolio. Digital or should it be hard copy?

5. If this is for the state, when is it due? Stagger any requirements to ensure you are not doing it all at once at the end of the year.

6. Ask your mentor (or support group) to help you put the portfolio together following these tips.

    a. Select the most meaningful samples from the artifact box or online folder. The examples you select should either relate to a standard or illustrate an area that is documenting proficiency. You should not keep samples that do not relate to required evidence needed unless you can make a connection to a teaching skill.

    b. Reflect on why this evidence is important and write a short caption or description for each artifact. The reflection is the explanation as to why this photo or sample of student work relates to teacher development. Connect the dots for the reader, so he can see how what you are displaying relates to standards.

    c. Ask your mentor for advice about an appropriate layout with the evidence, the sample artifacts and reflections. Organize a table of contents, place the philosophy statement up front, and place the reflections near the evidence.

7. Review the completed portfolio and acknowledge yourself for all you have done this year! Congratulations!

Companion Website

Some states or districts require a professional portfolio as evidence of completed evaluation standards, and others require documentation that you have met with a mentor for a number of hours during the year. All districts usually require a performance assessment that includes an observation of your teaching in the classroom. You need to ask your mentor what you need to show as evidence of completion. This book and the Novice Teacher Journal can serve as evidence of reflection and mentoring conversations. Consider dating the pages and using the digital calendar to document your meetings and observations.

If a portfolio is a requirement for your district or state, refer to Portfolio Development ideas in Figure 9 to guide the process. If a portfolio is not required, you may consider creating one to remember your year of teaching. If this is your first year, it is unlike any other year of teaching, and having a memory book with student photos and highlights of special activities is a worthwhile process.

Take the time to gather evidence as you move through the year so that you are not collecting it all at once in June when you are very busy. By using the Novice Teacher Journal, the companion website forms and calendar, and the book with tagged pages and notes, you will have evidence to share with any administrator that you indeed were mentored! If a more formal presentation is required, the portfolio option is one way to organize your evidence. The June chapter also includes suggestions for sharing your portfolio with others. Sharing your teaching practice with your mentor, your district administrators, other novice teachers, and yourself is an important way to acknowledge your growth and development as a teacher. This is your journey into teaching.

PART II

MONTH-BY-MONTH MENTORING
Being Mentored in Action

Why Do We Need a Mentoring Curriculum?

As a novice teacher, you are very busy all day and sometimes even overwhelmed by all you have to learn about teaching. If this is your first year of teaching, you may not even know what you are supposed to do each month. By having a month-by-month curriculum you can look ahead to see what will be expected of you at different times of the year. The monthly topics give you information in smaller pieces, so you can take it in and try some of the ideas. Use the content each month to empower you to ask your mentor questions and select the ACTs that would be most useful to you. Instead of waiting for a problem, which could turn into a crisis, be proactive and schedule short consistent meetings each month. Watch Video 2.1, *The First Years Matter,* on the companion website to hear how other novice teachers use this curriculum.

This book works best when your mentor is using the companion book, *Mentoring in Action,* because it provides you with a common language. However, if you are using it on your own to self-reflect or if you are a 2+ year teacher who was mentored last year, it is still valuable because it will help you align your teaching to the teaching standards. Using your own book to document your thinking, record notes, review topics for future months, and see what possible questions you might have that fully engages you in your teaching.

VIDEO 2.1

The First Years Matter

Figure 10   Developmental Continuum

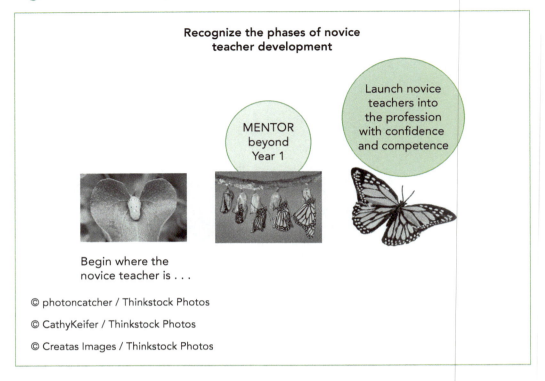

Recognize the phases of novice teacher development

MENTOR beyond Year 1

Launch novice teachers into the profession with confidence and competence

Begin where the novice teacher is . . .

© photoncatcher / Thinkstock Photos

© CathyKeifer / Thinkstock Photos

© Creatas Images / Thinkstock Photos

The butterfly image illustrates you emerging from the chrysalis to become the butterfly. This metamorphosis is the transformation that will take place in the beginning years of your teaching. The best way to differentiate and use this book is to begin with your strengths. What strengths do you bring to teaching? Draw on them now and build on what you already know to be true.

A Month-by-Month Cycle for Mentoring

Part II of the book is organized by months because that is how a school year operates. School districts often give novice teachers all the information they need for the entire year in a two- or

Figure 11   Cycle of Monthly Mentoring

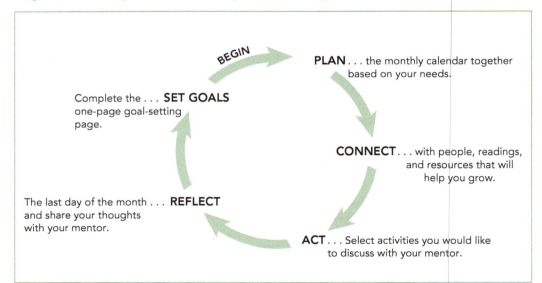

BEGIN

PLAN . . . the monthly calendar together based on your needs.

CONNECT . . . with people, readings, and resources that will help you grow.

ACT . . . Select activities you would like to discuss with your mentor.

The last day of the month . . . **REFLECT** and share your thoughts with your mentor.

Complete the . . . **SET GOALS** one-page goal-setting page.

three-day orientation. Novice teachers tell me that this is just too overwhelming, and not only does it create anxiety for them, but it is also confusing. This guide is organized to review and introduce topics throughout the school year in an organized way. Even with your mentor's best intentions, she may forget to review important teaching topics with you. With a curriculum, you are guaranteed to touch on the important topics as you look ahead and then review the topics each month. By having a curriculum, you can be proactive and ask questions when you need the information.

This book is organized around the following strategies: plan, connect, act, reflect, and set goals. This structure will provide focus as you move through the mentoring process each month. Each month begins with a chapter overview that includes guiding questions for the chapter as well as the national InTASC Standard that is featured. The overview also includes a novice teacher phase and a novice teacher affirmation as well as a quote from a student or novice teacher. This overview sets the tone for the chapter and gives you an idea of what you will be discussing with your mentor.

Figure 12 Organization of the Book

Mentoring Focus	Resources in the Book
PLAN to meet with your mentor weekly. This section includes sample questions, suggestions for being observed, and a calendar for scheduling meetings.	The first week of the month review the questions in the PLAN section and the content featured in the chapter. If your mentor is using the *Mentoring in Action* book, he may suggest pages he would like to focus on with you. The next two weeks of the month focus on ACT pages that are most meaningful and relevant to you. You can also watch videos alone or together and discuss them. The last meeting of the month is a time to REFLECT and SET GOALS using the forms provided. Short, in-person meetings at school or after school, e-mail dialogues, or phone appointments work well. Plan a time slot that works for both of you weekly and put it in your schedule!
CONNECT to existing resources.	This page provides a quick overview of ways you can connect to resources, student voices, hot topics, and the companion website. The ideas, videos, books, and articles will provide you with reminders for what you might use this year. Highlight the sections and tag the pages that stand out for you.
ACT through conversations with your mentor.	Review the Table of Contents and topics for ACTs each month. Select the pages that are most meaningful and useful each month. You don't have to complete all the pages or do the months in order. If you see a page in another chapter that applies to you now, read it now. Get to know where everything is so you can use the book as a resource. Notice that Classroom and Behavior Management Issues, Looking at Student Work, and Communicating With Parents offer topics each month because these recurring themes should be addressed consistently.
REFLECT with your mentor.	The last week of the month complete the REFLECT page and share your thoughts with your mentor or novice teacher support group. A Mindful Teaching Dilemma is also provided. This can be done with your mentor or with other novice teachers at a monthly meeting.
SET GOALS to move ahead.	This is an opportunity for you to acknowledge what you are doing well and articulate where you still have needs. Use this process to lead into your first weekly meeting for the next month. Adjust your PLAN calendar as needed to ensure you make some kind of contact with your mentor each week.

The Transformation of a Teacher

The words on the triangle in Figure 13 guide us to think about mentoring as a transformational experience. The ultimate goal for your mentor, and for the school district, is to transform you into that beautiful butterfly. Transformation is a process that takes time, and you may not see that ultimate change in your development in year one. Trust that the work you are doing with your mentor and your own self-reflection will influence your development over time. Students will benefit from your learning.

The heart is at the center of the triangle, because your heart will guide you to make the right decisions throughout the school year. You know why you chose to become a teacher. Remember that now as you begin your year of mentoring and reflection. The triangle offers you three ways to stay centered on your journey.

BALANCE. Maintain your balance through the year. Take your learning one step at a time. A teacher can't be at her best with students if she is burned out. You don't want to be that stressed out teacher! Learn how to develop your own social and emotional skills to stay healthy. Share this message of balance with your students in your classroom.

INSPIRE. Seek out teachers who inspire you. Observe the students who overcome challenges to come to school. Be the best teacher you can be for them. Listen to your mentor and learn from her wisdom as she shares the art and craft of teaching. Look into your own heart and touch the inspiration that led you to teaching. Find the joy in your work each day. Inspire others to do the same.

LEAD. First demonstrate your leadership skills in your classroom. Be a role model for your students and for other teachers in the school. Your words and actions are important. Think carefully before speaking and ask yourself, "How will my comment or response influence the students in my classroom?" Your professionalism using a mindfulness approach will influence your relationship with your mentor. Demonstrate your leadership beyond your classroom by stepping up to lead a novice teacher group. Sustain mentoring practices in your district by participating in the development of a formal mentoring plan that goes beyond the first year. This is the time to be a positive influence.

Watch Video 2.2, *Transformation of a Teacher,* available on the companion website, to hear a mentor talk about her observation of her mentees' development over a year. You are embarking upon a vocational journey. Your decision to become a teacher is just one of the many steps along the way. Your mindfulness disposition and intention to be the best teacher you can be is what will make the most difference to your development over time. Everything you do as a teacher has a ripple effect. Be intentional with your influence. Impact your students' lives in positive ways as you model professionalism.

VIDEO 2.2

The Transformation
of a Teacher

Figure 13 Transformation of a Teacher

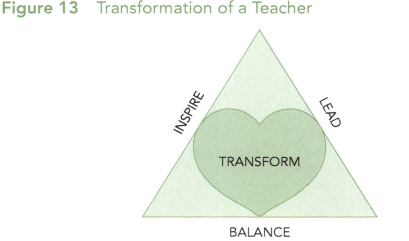

> **"**
> Good teachers care about their students, know who they are, and would go to any length to help them get the education they deserve.
> —HIGH SCHOOL STUDENT

NOVICE TEACHER PHASE: ANTICIPATION

"I'm so excited to have my own classroom!"

NOVICE TEACHER AFFIRMATION

I will intuitively listen to my needs and share them with my mentor.

AUGUST

ORIENTATION TO THE SCHOOL AND COMMUNITY
Resources and Values

GUIDING QUESTIONS

1. What do I bring to teaching and how can my mentor help me? The **Reflect ACTivities** will provide ways to think about your skills and qualities.

2. How will I learn about important school information? The **Introduce ACTivities** provide you with topics you may want to share.

3. How can I prepare for the first weeks of school? The **Prepare ACTivities** provide you with information and conversation starters to focus your time.

Interstate Teacher Assessment and Support Consortium—InTASC Standards

Review all 10 of the InTASC Standards on page 5 in Part I. On the front page of each month, you will find the standards that relate to that chapter's focus. If you are being supported by a mentor, discuss how your mentoring conversations align with teacher evaluation requirements. If you are using this book on your own, review the standards that will be used to assess your growth. A sample Evaluation Alignment Tool is available on page 6 in Part I.

Chapter Overview

Whether you are a first-time-in-the-classroom teacher, a new-to-district teacher, or a 2+ year teacher who wants to be more proficient, you will find this book, *The First Years Matter,* to be a useful tool. If your mentor is using the *Mentoring in Action* book's curriculum, you will find that the monthly chapters align by ACTs, so you can easily collaborate. If you are using the book on your own as a reflective tool, you can pace yourself and skip around finding the topics that are most meaningful to you.

Being mentored and reflecting on your practice while you are in your first classroom is both exciting and exhausting work. You may feel isolated and alone right now if this is your first year. Document your journey into teaching by completing the pages in this book as you go through the school year. If you do have a district mentor, use the questions on the PLAN pages to frame your discussions so that you don't waste valuable time. This book can also be used as a personal journal to capture your thoughts throughout the year. Use the Novice Teacher Journal on the companion website to record your reflections for each month. At the end of the year, you will have an opportunity to review them and see how much you have grown.

August is an opportunity for you to meet other beginning teachers in the school and the district. As you read the chapter, find out who the other novice teachers are by asking your mentor or other teachers. If you are not a member of this community, explore the cultures of the students and their families. Read the mission statement of the school and find out what the leaders value. Reflect on why you accepted a position at this school. Is this your dream job? Why or why not?

Create a survival guide for yourself (see the ACT on page 36 for this month) and learn as much as you can about the school and community now. You will soon discover that there is a lot more to teaching than preparing lessons. If this is your first classroom, you may be very excited to get started and want to ignore all this paper work and school procedures. Be patient, be resourceful, and ask questions, so you can get organized. If this is your second or third year, you have discovered what you didn't know and are most likely doing things differently this year. Use these August pages as a review and to go deeper into your teaching for this month. Your Novice Teacher Affirmation for this month is, *I will intuitively listen to my needs and share them with my mentor.* If you do not have a formal mentor, ask another teacher to help you this year, or create a novice teacher support group.

VIDEO 2.3

Mentoring in Action: August Chapter Introduction

As the student says in the quote, good teachers help students get the education they deserve. Your role as a teacher is to learn how to teach most effectively to all of your students. Speak up and get the help you need to be the best teacher you can be. If you are a 2+ year teacher using this book for the first or second time, it is an opportunity to deepen your reflections and refine your teaching practices. You also may still need help and should not be afraid to ask for it.

Skim through the entire book so that you will know how it is organized and what topics it includes each month. Feel free to pick and choose activities that relate to your development. Watch and listen to novice teachers who have used *The First Years Matter* on the companion website or scan the QR code on a mobile device. Watch and listen to a mentor share her insights in Video 2.3, *Mentoring in Action: August Chapter Introduction*, on the companion website or scan the QR code on a mobile device.

Novice Teacher Journal

One way to plan your month is to assess where you are right now. Writing in your Novice Teacher Journal will help you document what you are feeling and how to focus your teaching. A digital version of the journal is available on the companion website.

Directions: Review the chapter opening page and the overview for this month. How do this month's topic, the quotes, phase, and affirmation relate to you right now? How are you feeling as you prepare for the school year to begin? What do you feel confident about? Where do you need some help?

Use your journal to record your thoughts, feelings, and questions in a free-flowing narrative. This page is for your personal reflection; it does not need to be shared with your mentor unless you choose to do so. A digital version of this page is available in the Novice Teacher Journal on the companion website. At the end of the year, you can review your monthly reflections to see how much you have grown.

If you are a 2+ year teacher, you are aware of the expectations for teaching in June. Your journal entry will delve deeper into your practice using the same questions.

August Entry Date_____

Today I feel . . .

_____

_____

_____

I am confident in the areas of . . .

_____

_____

_____

I need some help . . .

_____

_____

_____

Companion
Website

Questions for Participating in Mentoring Conversations

Participating in a mentoring conversation requires you to be fully engaged. It requires listening and being open to what your mentor is sharing. This means you need to think about the questions you have and how to ask them. It does not mean you have to do exactly what your mentor recommends, but it does mean you will reflect on the conversations and think about what makes sense for you. If you are a 2+ year teacher, these may not all apply to you; however, there may be a question you would like to revisit.

Check the questions that you would like to discuss with your mentor or other teachers in your school.

Your Possible Questions

1. How do I create a community of learners? What does that look like?

2. Who are my students and their families?

3. What do I need to know about the community?

4. What do I need to know about this school and its procedures for opening a school year and a new classroom?

5. What values, expectations, or cultural norms are in operation in this school and the community?

6. Is there a written mission statement for the school?

7. Do you have any suggestions for me as I set up my first classroom?

8. How do I get materials for my classroom and my students?

9. Are there any restrictions or expectations for setting up my classroom space?

Other questions I have . . .

Be Prepared: Your Mentor May Also Ask You Questions!

Anticipate Your Mentor's Questions

1. What do you already know about this community?

2. What are you planning to do to prepare your room, and why are you doing that?

3. Do you have any experience setting up a classroom?

4. What can I do to assist you right now that would reduce your anxiety?

Meetings and Observations

Plan brief weekly meetings with your mentor. The ACTs in this chapter serve as mentoring conversation starters and can also be used to assess or review what you may already know about a given topic.

Plan to meet at times that allow you to have quality time together in a place without interruptions. Knowing when you will meet each week reduces anxiety for you. You will find that you look forward to regularly scheduled meetings especially if they are short. Use this calendar to document your meetings and invite your mentor to schedule classroom visits to see you in action. There are many videos in this book and also in your mentor's *Mentoring in Action* book. Consider scheduling time to watch the videos together and have a discussion. A digital version of this calendar (August Calendar.pdf) is available on the companion website.

Would you like to observe your mentor teach before she watches you? Ask her if you can visit her classroom this month. Use the observation form, "A Novice Teacher Observes a Mentor," on the companion website to guide your observation. Schedule a postconference to discuss any questions you have. Will your mentor be observing you this year? Schedule tentative dates in your calendar.

August Calendar

MONDAY	TUESDAY	WEDNESDAY	THURSDAY	FRIDAY

Use this calendar to PLAN the month with your mentor as well as to document meetings.

CONNECT to Additional Resources

CONNECT to School and District Resources

What resources exist in your school and community that could assist you in setting up your classroom? What did you write in your journal that you need this month? How can your mentor help?

CONNECT With Colleagues, Parents, and Families

Who in the school building (experienced teachers, other beginning teachers, custodians, secretaries) may be able to help you?

How do you introduce yourself to the parents and families? Is there a protocol? Ask your mentor.

CONNECT to Student Voices

What does *respect* look like in a classroom, and how can you ensure that you include this important quality as you create a community of learners? Review the ideas on the form "What Does Respect Look Like in the Classroom," available on the companion website, for specific ways to integrate respect.

CONNECT to Education Hot Topics

Use portable devices for learning! Back to school means school supplies. Portable devices are now part of the student's backpack. How will you use these devices appropriately? Discuss the role of social media and its proper use in school with your mentor. Review Hot Topics on the We Are Teachers website to identify the strategies that work best.

CONNECT With the Companion Website

Video links, forms for this chapter, a featured book, and other resources by the author are located at resources.corwin.com/mentoringinaction.

The First ACT!

Differentiating Mentoring Conversations

Teaching is complex work, and you can easily become overwhelmed. It is appropriate to customize your mentoring conversations so that your mentor is responding to your needs and skills.

Directions: Discuss the prompts with your mentor or think about them on your own. Refer to your state or district teaching standards to note a common language for teaching and summarize your key ideas in each box. Skim the ACTS for this month and decide which topics are most relevant to your needs this month. If you are a 2+ year teacher, use this template as a self-reflection or share it in your novice teacher support group.

Name _____ Date _____

Monthly Needs Assessment

1. What is going well in your classroom right now?	3. What would you like to improve or enhance in your practice this month?
2. How do you know your practice is working? What is your evidence of success?	4. Review the ACT overview of possible conversations for this month with your mentor. What would you like to focus on this month?

A digital version of this template (Monthly Needs Assessment Sample With Standards.pdf) is available on the companion website. Keep a copy of this assessment in your professional file.

Companion Website

Overview of the ACTs for August Conversations

Directions: Skim the ACTivities listed here and complete the pages that will forward your learning. If you are a 2+ year teacher, revisit any ACTs you already completed or try some new ACTs to stretch your thinking. Digital copies of some of the ACTs are available on the companion website.

Key Question Topic	ACTivities	PAGE
Reflect	ACT 1 **Preparing to Be Mentored**	31
Reflect	ACT 2 **Getting to Know Your Mentor**	32
Introduce	ACT 3 **How Will You Contribute to Your School?**	33
Introduce	ACT 4 **Introducing the School and District**	34
Introduce	ACT 5 **Getting to Know the Students and Their Families**	35
Introduce	ACT 6 **Creating a Survival Packet: What Novice Teachers Need to Know Now**	36
Prepare	ACT 7 **Building a Mentoring Relationship**	37
Prepare	ACT 8 **The Importance of Lesson Planning**	38
Prepare	ACT 9 **Daily Lesson Plans for Student Success**	39
Prepare	ACT 10 **The First Days and Weeks of School**	40

Preparing to Be Mentored

Key Question: How will you participate fully in mentoring?

Directions: Reflect on your previous experiences of being mentored or mentoring someone else. You may have mentored a student in school or a senior citizen as a volunteer. Or perhaps you had a mentor in a previous job because you are a career changer. Mentoring requires a commitment on your part. Your mentor can help you only if you are open to suggestions and willing to honestly share your needs. Record your reflections on this page or use the Novice Teacher Journal provided on the companion website to type your responses.

1. What is your experience of mentoring others?

2. What is your experience of being mentored?

3. Name a mentor in your life (they do not have to relate to education) who was helpful to you. Why?

4. Is mentoring a requirement in your district? How do you feel about that?

5. How will you approach being mentored? (i.e., what is your commitment to listening and taking suggestions?)

6. How can a mentor support you?

7. If you are using this book *without* a formal mentor, how will you self-mentor to get the most out of this curriculum?

8. Based on previous mentoring experiences, what do you need to do to fully and successfully participate in mentoring in action?

Companion
Website

Getting to Know Your Mentor

Key Question: What would you like to know about your mentor?

Directions: Review the questions below and check the ones you would like to ask your mentor. At a scheduled meeting or in an informal setting, have a conversation about your mentor's experiences and beliefs about teaching. Use this as an opportunity to learn your mentor's background and also the requirements of the school district mentoring program.

1. Why did you become a teacher? Share your story.

2. How many years have you been teaching? Where?

3. What do you see as the strengths of this school and community?

4. What is expected of me as a novice teacher in this district?

5. What challenges should I expect at the school this year? Why do you say that?

6. What is your role with me? How often do we meet? Do I bring questions to you? Can I e-mail you?

7. What is your job description for being a mentor?

8. Is there any paperwork I need to complete to document that I was mentored?

9. What do you love about teaching?

10. What would you like to share with me?

Companion
Website

How Will You Contribute to Your School?

Key Question: What do I bring to teaching that I can share with others?

Directions: Beginning teachers bring energy, passion, and new ideas into the classroom and the school. Even though you may not feel totally confident yet, you have so many skills to share and use in the classroom. Review your strengths and acknowledge what you bring to teaching. Your mentor will want to learn from you too! Respond to the prompts below in a narrative format and e-mail your completed profile to your mentor. Don't be afraid to share! A digital copy is available on the companion website.

Novice Teacher Profile

1. Teacher Preparation

   A. Describe your preparation for teaching. What path did you take to become certified? Describe one course that you took in your preparation at the college that stands out for you as being a useful preparation for teaching and why.

   B. List your previous experiences in schools as a student teacher or previous teaching experiences.

2. Skills and Experiences

   A. Do you speak a world language? Explain.

   B. Do you or have you played or coached sports? Explain.

   C. Where have you traveled? Why did you visit these places?

   D. Do you have musical, drama, or any arts ability? Explain.

   E. What is your level of proficiency with computers and other technology?

   F. Other hobbies?

3. Life and Professional Goals

   A. Where do you see yourself in five years? ten years? twenty years?

   B. Why did you choose teaching at this time?

4. Personal Joys and Strengths

   A. What do you most enjoy in your life?

   B. What are you really good at?

5. What would you like me to know about you?

6. What would you like to know about me?

Introducing the School and District

Key Question: Who and what do you need to know about the school and district to be successful?

Directions: Knowing the important facts about the school, the district, and who is important to your successful integration into the school culture is crucial to your success. Find the responses to these questions by using the school website; talking with secretaries, custodians, or teachers; or reviewing school printed materials. Walk around the school and see how many answers you can find! A digital version can be found on the companion website. Don't forget to ask your mentor to introduce you to the important people on this list!

School Scavenger Hunt

1. What is the name of the school, and why does it have this name? How old is the school? Also list the phone, e-mail, and website address.

2. How many students are enrolled in this school? What is the diversity of students by ethnicity? What are the languages spoken?

3. What are the official school hours? Are there recess times for students? What is the schedule for classes? When do teachers arrive at school and leave at the end of the day? What is the lunch period for teachers? Do you have lesson planning time? Will you have duties?

4. Is public transportation available to the school? If so, what is the schedule?

5. Is there a school theme or mission of the school? How is it displayed?

6. How is the school organized? What is the number of teachers at each grade level and in content areas?

7. How many experienced teachers are working at this school? How many teachers are in their first three years of teaching?

8. Who is the principal and who is the assistant principal? Who is the superintendent? (spelling of their names counts!)

9. How many specialist teachers are at the school? Will your students participate in these classes?

10. How will special education influence your teaching schedule? Are there paraprofessional aides?

11. Who are the secretaries and custodians you should get to know?

12. Is there a parent volunteer program? Will it relate to you?

13. Are there any special programs or activities at this school or in this district?

14. What are teachers most proud of in this school? (You may ask several teachers and compare.)

15. How does this school's image and reputation relate to other schools in the district and the state?

Is there anything else you would like to know about the school or district? Ask your mentor!

Getting to Know the Students and Their Families

Key Question: How can you learn about the students and their families?

Directions: Getting to know the students and the local community is important, especially if you have moved from another state and are unfamiliar with this town. Review the ideas listed here and be prepared to discuss your ideas with your mentor. Feel free to add your own ideas to this list. A digital version is on the companion website.

Ways to Introduce Yourself and Learn About Students and Families

1. Interviewing students—One way to find out about the school is to talk with students. They are usually hanging around the school in August waiting for it to start! Ask students what they like about this school, what they find challenging, and how teachers can help them learn. Create other interview questions to find out what you would like to learn about this school. The students tell it like it is! Don't be surprised by their responses!

2. Interviewing Parents—Where there are students there may be parents. Take this opportunity to introduce yourself and ask the parents about the school and the district. This simple informal research will give you lots of insight into the perspective of the parents and what they think about the school.

3. Observe the Community—If you don't live in this town, you need to learn about it. Some orientation programs provide a tour of the town and all the schools in the district. If that is not available, take a drive or a bus and see what this community looks like. Note where the schools are located within the town. Where is the downtown area? Is there a public library? What do the neighborhoods look like, and how does that impact the schools? Are there other resources you can use in the town? Museums? Recycle centers?

4. Review the School Website—This will help you find the answers for the Scavenger Hunt in ACT 4. You need to know how the website is used in this district and if it is important to you.

5. Write a letter to the students—Introduce yourself before the school year begins or during the first week of school. Share your background, your interests, and what you are looking forward to!

6. Write a letter to the parents and/or guardians—Share what you will be doing this year and how they can reach you if they have any questions. Be sure to include how excited you are to be teaching.

Are there other ways you can learn about students and families? Discuss them with your mentor!

AUGUST

Creating a Survival Packet

Key Question: What do you need to know right now?

Directions: Surviving the first year of teaching is a goal for most novice teachers. If this is your second or third year, you know now what you wished you had known in year one! Ask your mentor to help you create a practical survival packet that will be useful to you all year. Watch Video 2.4, *Creating a Survival Packet*, to see a mentor and novice talking about the survival packet.

Survival Packet Important Information

1. ***School and District Materials and Where to Find Them***

   - Schedules (daily, weekly, block, holiday) and student and school handbooks with policies

   - Mission statements, vision statements, curriculum guides

   - Class lists (how to get them and who creates them) and list of faculty and e-mails

   - Report cards, parent communication, discipline policies, and policy for reporting abuse or neglect

   - Professional development schedule and school closing policies (emergency and snow closings)

2. ***Buzz Words (here is a sample of education jargon)***

   - BBST, ESL, ELL, IEP, AYP, KWL, AFT and NEA, Title I, InTASC

   - Words or initials you have heard that you don't know

3. ***Procedures and School Culture Protocols***

   - Fire drill and other building exiting procedures

   - Protocols and expectations that are not written (how teachers get lunch and where they eat)

   - Sending students to the nurse (from colds to crisis—how to know the difference)

   - Getting support for students in crisis (home problems that students bring to school)

   - Guidelines for referring students for misbehavior (where do they go? what do you write?)

   - Supervisory duties and expectations for novice teachers (hall duty, cafeteria, recess duty, bus duty)

   - How and where to make copies for lessons and take out library books

4. ***Building Floor Plan and School Organization***

   - Map of school with room numbers and exits clearly labeled (also nurse, office, workrooms, bathrooms, staff lounges) and map of school yard, where buses drop off, and entrances

5. ***Teacher Union Information and State Licensing Information***

   - Reviewing the teacher contract and state requirements

   - Reviewing union benefits

VIDEO 2.4

Creating a Survival Packet

Companion Website

Building a Mentoring Relationship

Key Question: How can you get the most out of being mentored?

Directions: Review the ideas and use any that relate to you and your mentor. Discuss the self-assessment to find out how you assess each area listed. Rate yourself using a scale ranging from 1 *(low)* to 5 *(high)* for each of the following areas:

1. **Self-Assessment**

	Competence I have experience . . .	Confidence I feel . . .
Setting up a classroom		
Introducing myself to students and parents		
Lesson and unit planning		
Creating and implementing classroom routines		
Managing disruptive behavior of students		
Working with students from other cultures		
Learning how to navigate school culture		
Other topics		

VIDEO 2.5

Design Alliance

2. Watch Video 2.5, *Design Alliance*, with your mentor and discuss the ideas that are presented.

3. Find out if the teacher preparation program at your university provides any support for novice teachers and reach out to those support systems. Share what you find with your mentor.

Companion Website

The Importance of Lesson Planning

Key Question: What do you need to know about planning effective lessons?

Directions: Review the key ideas on this page and discuss the most relevant topics with your mentor or reflect on them alone.

Lesson Planning Overview

1. Review lesson and unit planning requirements.

2. Discuss specific ways lesson planning can minimize student distraction and engage learners.

3. Illustrate how school and state standards are supposed to be reflected in lesson plans.

4. Share daily plans in short form as well as long form plans that are used at your school.

5. Review curriculum and expectations for the novice teacher to design unit plans.

6. Share your specific plans for the first days of school with your mentor.

7. Ask your mentor to share his experience of daily planning and show you some plans.

8. Co-plan with the mentor to ensure the first days of school include necessary introduction activities.

9. Skim the October chapter to see more lesson and unit planning.

10. If you are a 2+ year teacher compare your plans to last year's plans.

Companion Website

Daily Lesson Plans for Student Success

Key Question: What do you need to know about daily lesson planning?

Directions: Review the key ideas on this page in a conversation with your mentor or reflect on them alone. An effective teacher knows that the lesson plan is a way of organizing information the students need to learn. Use these ideas to review the important questions a teacher needs to think about when developing a plan. Review a sample lesson plan you have developed and see if you can answer these questions.

Lesson Planning Questions

1. Why am I teaching this lesson?

2. Which standards am I addressing? Where are they noted on the plan?

3. Am I presenting the content in a way that is relevant to students?

4. Am I including higher order thinking in my activities?

5. What do I want all students to learn?

6. How will I modify for special students?

7. What assessment tools will I use to measure success?

8. What is the motivation for students to stay engaged?

9. How much teacher talking time is in this plan (i.e., lecture)?

10. Do students have an opportunity to practice and share? How long?

11. Is there an opportunity for students to reflect on their learning and set goals?

12. What routines and systems are in place to minimize student distractions?

Companion Website

The First Days and Weeks of School

Key Question: How can you prepare for the first days and weeks of school?

Directions: Review the four ideas on this page with your mentor or reflect on them alone. Add any other ideas or resources that you need to be successful.

1. *Design Classroom Space*

Draw a floor plan of your room. Include teacher's desk and student seats. Include traffic flow and make sure all students can see the teacher with this plan. Share your floor plan with your mentor.

2. *Establish Effective Routines*

Discuss the importance of routines with your mentor. Ask her why they need to be established on the first days of school. Ask the mentor to share her routines with you. Discuss how you will share these routines with your students.

3. *First Day Lesson Plans*

Ask your mentor what you should teach in the beginning days of school. Ask her to share the lesson plans she has used on the first days of classes. How does she learn students' names. Does she take photos of each of her students?

4. *Materials and Supplies*

Ask your mentor where to get books, supplies, and materials for the first weeks of school, so you will be prepared for the students.

You will gain competence if you present yourself with confidence in the first weeks of school. Ask your mentor for tips for maintaining your balance in those hectic first weeks of school.

August Novice Teacher Reflections

Directions: Complete any of these prompts to summarize your experience this month. Add your own prompts to the blank stems. Compare and share your reflections with your mentor or other novice teachers in your support group. You can also complete these reflections in your Novice Teacher Journal.

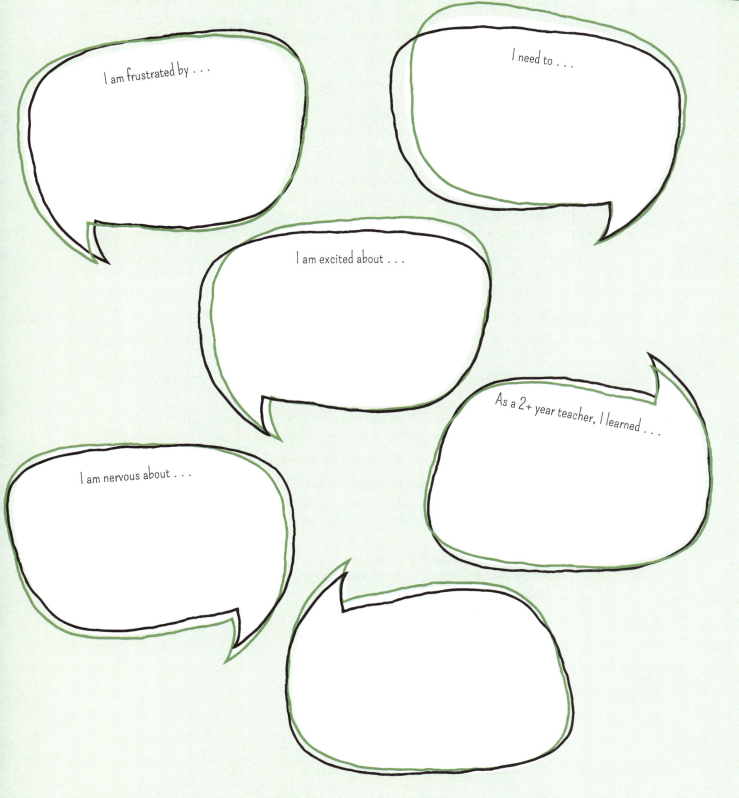

I am frustrated by . . .

I need to . . .

I am excited about . . .

As a 2+ year teacher, I learned . . .

I am nervous about . . .

Using Mindfulness to Explore Teaching Dilemmas

Teaching is complex, and often there are not clear answers to situations that arise while you are being mentored. The teaching dilemmas introduced at the end of each month in the REFLECT section may not always apply to you; however, the process of reflecting on this dilemma will help you think about what you might do if this did happen to you. Sometimes when a situation arises that we didn't anticipate, we react and say things before we think. This journal process will allow you to "pause" and think about what you would like to say next. These dilemmas are useful for mentoring conversation starters, novice teacher support group discussions, and personal reflection.

Dilemma 1: Choosing to Be a Teacher

You decided to become a teacher because you love teaching. It has been your passion since elementary school. You are ready to begin in your first classroom, and you start to hear how challenging it is to teach in this school. You meet your mentor who is competent and helpful, and you are already feeling overwhelmed by all the things you need to learn. You are afraid you might be over your head. You find out many novice teachers have left the district, and now you are getting nervous. Your parents and friends have questioned your decision to teach and said, "You are so smart, why are you going to be a teacher?" You are questioning your choice to teach. If you are a 2+ year teacher, how does this dilemma relate to you now? *What do you do?*

Respond to these prompts in your Novice Teacher Journal, available on the companion website.

1. State the dilemma as clearly as possible in one sentence if you can.

2. What decision do you need to make in regard to this situation?

3. Write about the emotions that come up for you that relate to this situation. If you have two choices, write how the emotions might be different.

4. Stop and reread what you have written. Underline any key words or phrases that stand out for you.

5. Soften your eyes or close them and take three deep breaths. Ask yourself, what am I missing that I have not noticed. Write that down in your journal.

6. How can your mentor help you? Write your reflection in your journal.

7. If you are truly stuck, bring your dilemma to another novice teacher in their second or third year of teaching. Ask him or her to listen and to ask you questions to clarify your dilemma. Ask her not to give advice, just to ask you questions to help you clarify your feelings and next steps.

8. How do you feel about this dilemma now? All dilemmas are not resolved! This is a process of clarifying and understanding how you feel and how you might proceed in the future.

Directions: Complete the goal-setting processes alone or with your mentor. Write your responses on this page or in your Novice Teacher Journal, available on the companion website. If you are a 2+ year teacher, reflect on how you are growing from year to year.

1. *Goal for Improving Your Teaching Practices*

   - Review the PLAN–CONNECT–ACT–REFLECT pages you completed in this chapter with your mentor. Look ahead to September ACTs to see what you may focus on to continue your development.

   - Acknowledge what you are learning. Be specific! Compliment yourself for doing something well!

   - Reflect on your teaching this month. What stood out as effective? What will you do differently next month?

   - Agree on ONE goal with your mentor to reinforce your learning for next month.

   - Goal:

2. *Goal to Support Your Social and Emotional Well-Being*

   - Discuss any challenges you may be facing right now. Challenges often bring stress.

   - Don't ignore any signs of stress! Pay attention and learn ways to manage your stress. Using mindfulness practices can help reduce stress. To learn more about mindfulness and managing stress, watch the mindfulness video (Kelly McGonigle's TED Talk "How to Make Stress Your Friend") and read the *Benefits of Mindfulness* article and discuss it together. Both are available on the companion website.

   - Goal:

> "
> A good teacher is someone who is helpful, thoughtful, smart, knows how to teach, and loves kids.
>
> —THIRD-GRADE STUDENT

NOVICE TEACHER PHASE: NERVOUS AND READY

"I feel prepared to teach, but I don't know what to do the first day."

NOVICE TEACHER AFFIRMATION

I ask for what I need to be successful.

SEPTEMBER

BEGINNING THE SCHOOL YEAR SUCCESSFULLY

Creating a Community of Learners in the Classroom

GUIDING QUESTIONS

1. How do I create a community of learners in my classroom? The *Relationship ACTivities* provide ways to approach this task.
2. How will I learn how to implement routines in my classroom? The *Routines ACTivities* offer you ideas to discuss with your mentor.
3. How will I learn ways to implement classroom and behavior management routines and look at student work systematically? Use the *Student ACTivities* as a way to begin to focus on these topics.
4. How will I reach out to parents? Use the *Communication ACTivity* as a way to focus on ways to connect with parents and families.

Interstate Teacher Assessment and Support Consortium—InTASC Standards

This month will focus on InTASC Standards 1 and 2. Discuss these with your mentor.

For the complete list of standards go to page 5 in Part I of this book.

- **Standard 1 Learner Development**

The teacher understands how learners grow and develop, recognizing that patterns of learning and development vary individually within and across the cognitive, linguistic, social, emotional, and physical areas, and designs and implements developmentally appropriate and challenging learning experiences.

- **Standard 2 Learning Differences**

The teacher uses understanding of individual differences and diverse cultures and communities to ensure inclusive learning environments that enable each learner to meet high standards.

Chapter Overview

A wise person once said, *"Wisdom is not knowing what to do ultimately; it is knowing what to do next."* As a novice teacher, you will work with a mentor and perhaps a small group of novice teachers in your school or district. You need to be open to building relationships with not only your students but your colleagues as well. Some of the teachers will be informally assisting you, and others may be paid to help you set up your first classroom. If you have an assigned official mentor, it is your responsibility to work to create a positive and trusting relationship. The mentor will be working to do the same. Be open to learning new ideas and ways to approach the school year. You don't have to copy everything your mentor does, but you should be open to listening and asking questions about why she or he approaches her or his school year a certain way.

Each novice teacher in the school will have different needs based on their previous experiences and teacher preparation. What do you need? How can you minimize the anxiety you are feeling in September so that you can maximize student learning in your classroom this month?

As a beginning teacher, you must have conversations with your mentor that relate to building student learning communities in the classroom. Relationships with students are crucial to your success in the classroom. Students are disruptive if they are bored or if they feel the teacher doesn't know them. By relating to students, you can maximize student learning and minimize disruptions in your classroom.

Your mentor serves as a guide, but she will not be telling you what to do. She can offer suggestions, and you can try ideas, but ultimately it is your decision to choose what works best in your classroom. You will have questions, emotional ups and downs, and lots of ideas you want to try out this month and this year. Listen to the many ways your mentors and colleagues plan for the opening of school and explore the options with them. Mentoring is not about someone *telling* you what to do; it is about *creating* opportunities where you can discover what to do in your own classroom. It is also okay to follow exactly what your mentor is doing this month. After all, you are just getting started; you may not know what to do.

Learn to listen to what your mentor says and ask questions. Trust yourself and be honest about what you feel is right for your classroom. Your affirmation this month is, "I ask for what I need to be successful." Think about how it feels to ask for help and recognize that it is okay to get help.

Follow the PLAN, CONNECT, ACT, REFLECT, and SET GOALS sections in this chapter to guide your mentoring conversations with your mentor and your personal reflections in your Novice Teacher Journal. Watch and listen to a mentor share her insights in Video 2.6, *Mentoring in Action: September Chapter Introduction*, on the companion website or scan the QR code on a mobile device.

VIDEO 2.6

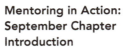

Mentoring in Action: September Chapter Introduction

Novice Teacher Journal

One way to plan your month is to assess where you are right now. Writing in your Novice Teacher Journal will help you document what you are feeling and how to focus your teaching. A digital version of the journal is available on the companion website.

Directions: Review the chapter cover page and the overview for this month. How do this month's topic, the quotes, phase, and affirmation, relate to you right now? How are you feeling as you prepare for the school year to begin? What do you feel confident about? Where do you need some help?

Use your journal to record your thoughts, feelings, and questions in a free-flowing narrative. This page is for your personal reflection; it does not need to be shared with your mentor unless you choose to do so. At the end of the year, you can review your monthly reflections to see how much you have grown.

September Entry Date_____

Today I feel . . .

_____

_____

_____

I am confident in the areas of . . .

_____

_____

_____

I need some help . . .

_____

_____

_____

Companion
Website

Questions for Participating in Mentoring Conversations

Sometimes you don't know what to ask your mentor because you don't know what you don't know! Review this list and choose some questions that are useful to you. How will your mentor respond? Will you schedule a face-to-face meeting, a phone appointment, or send an e-mail? What works best for both of you? Reflect on your mentor's responses and think about what works for you. If you are a 2+ year teacher, these may not all apply to you; however, there may be a question you would like to revisit.

Your Possible Questions

1. How do students learn at this grade level?

    - How many of my students need support in English language learning, and what should I do to help them integrate socially and academically?

    - Can you share some successful ways for setting up a classroom in September?

    - What are self-motivating strategies for students?

    - What do I do if a student misbehaves?

Other questions I have . . .

Anticipate Your Mentor's Questions

1. What is your understanding of child/adolescent development?

2. For which grade level did you complete your student teaching?

3. How confident are you at this time?

4. What can I do to assist you right now to minimize your anxiety?

Meetings and Observations

Plan brief weekly meetings with your mentor. The ACTs in this chapter serve as mentoring conversation starters and can also be used to assess or review what you may already know about a given topic.

Plan to meet at times that allow you to have quality time together in a place without interruptions. Use this calendar to schedule your meetings and classroom visits to ensure they will happen! Include watching videos or reading pages in *The First Years Matter* as part of your *PLAN*. A digital version of this calendar (September Calendar.pdf) is available on the companion website.

Invite your mentor to visit your classroom. A before school or after school visit is an opportunity for you to share how the room is organized as well to show and tell your mentor what you have done so far. Schedule this visit early to be sure it happens.

September Calendar

MONDAY	TUESDAY	WEDNESDAY	THURSDAY	FRIDAY

Use this calendar to PLAN the month with your mentor as well as to document meetings.

Companion
Website

CONNECT to Additional Resources

CONNECT to School and District Resources

What resources exist in your school and community that could assist you in beginning the school year successfully?

CONNECT With Colleagues and Parents

Who are the teachers you want to know? Ask your mentor to introduce you.

Who or what agency in the community could provide resources or support for no or low cost?

How will you learn about any nontraditional family models that may exist within your school and district? (e.g., grandparents, single mothers or fathers, legal guardians, same gender parents, etc.)

CONNECT to Student Voices

How are students showing up in your classroom? When your mentor walks into your classroom, what evidence of students will he see? Are their names are on the walls, photos posted, or student work displayed on the wall of fame? Seeing students "in the room" when they are not physically in the room demonstrates the visible mark that students have in the classroom. Discuss this important topic with your mentor, using the form titled, "How Do Students *Show Up* in the Classroom?" available on the companion website.

CONNECT to Education Hot Topics

Organize your space! As you organize your classroom, discuss the ways the space can be used most effectively. Search for online tips such as "easy ways to make your space work for you and your students." Explore articles online to find out how wall color, lighting, and eliminating clutter influence the classroom environment. Share what you find with your mentor.

CONNECT With the Companion Website

Video links, forms for this chapter, a featured book and other resources by the author are located at resources.corwin.com/mentoringinaction

Companion Website

The First ACT!

Differentiating Mentoring Conversations

Teaching is complex work, and you can easily become overwhelmed. It is appropriate to customize your mentoring conversations so that your mentor is responding to your needs and skills.

Directions: Discuss the prompts with your mentor or think about them on your own. Refer to your state or district teaching standards to note a common language for teaching and summarize your key ideas in each box. Skim the ACTs for this month and decide which topics are most relevant to your needs this month.

Name_____ Date _____

Monthly Needs Assessment

1. What is going well in your classroom right now?	3. What would you like to improve or enhance in your practice this month?
2. How do you know your practice is working? What is your evidence of success?	4. Review the ACT overview of possible conversations for this month with your mentor. What would you like to focus on this month?

A digital version of this template (Monthly Needs Assessment Sample With Standards.pdf) is available on the companion website. Keep a copy of this assessment in your professional file.

Companion Website

SEPTEMBER

Overview of the ACTs for September Conversations

Directions: Skim the ACTivities listed here and complete the pages that will forward your learning. If you are a 2+ year teacher, revisit any ACTs you already completed or try some new ACTs to stretch your thinking. Digital copies of some of the ACTs are available on the companion website.

Key Question Topic	ACTivities	PAGE
Relationship	ACT 1 **Creating a Community of Learners in the Classroom**	53
Relationship	ACT 2 **Getting to Know the Students**	54
Relationship	ACT 3 **Creating a Classroom Profile**	55
Relationship	ACT 4 **Learning How Students Learn**	56
Routines	ACT 5 **Establishing and Implementing Routines**	57
Routines	ACT 6 **Rules, Rewards, and Consequences**	58
Routines	ACT 7 **Learning School Procedures**	59
Students	ACT 8 **Classroom and Behavior Management Issues**	60
Students	ACT 9 **Looking at Student Work Together**	61
Communication	ACT 10 **Communicating With Parents**	62

Creating a Community of Learners in the Classroom

Key Question: What should you review about building a learning community?

Directions: Review the list of ideas on this page and choose the topics that are most relevant to your learning. Discuss your ideas with your mentor.

1. How does an effective teacher include students of other cultures in the community?

2. What does respect look like in the classroom, and how does a novice teacher create a respectful classroom?

3. Invite your mentor to share what she knows about team building and student communities.

4. How can student sharing create a safe and respectful classroom? Discuss this idea. Start the day or class with five minutes of student sharing time. Rationale: Students come to school with lots of issues related to their personal lives. Getting to know each other, learning how to listen, and respecting the lives of others can enhance a classroom community.

5. How can student partners help to build a spirit of teamwork? Discuss this idea. Allow students to work together, sit together, and support each other in learning. Rationale: Students want to talk to each other. By trying to keep them quiet all day, we attempt an impossible task. Letting students talk to a partner allows them to release energy and stay on task. By organizing sharing partners, novice teachers can structure student talking time and use it to create a sharing classroom. For example, when a student is absent, his or her partner can collect all the work and share.

6. How can learning teams and small groups make school more engaging for students who want to interact? Teams can work on projects, create team slogans, and challenge each other in academic contests. Why is it important to rotate teams periodically? Rationale: Teamwork is more fun for some students and teaches students how to work together to achieve learning goals.

7. How can student compliments encourage kindness? Students who give each other compliments at the end of the day as part of the teacher's routine feel good when they leave school and want to come back the next day. Rationale for this activity: Everyone likes to hear that his classmates notice what he is doing to build a community in the classroom. Discuss how the teacher has to model the compliment process by giving compliments to students. Positive words create caring communities.

Companion Website

Getting to Know the Students

Key Question: How can you learn about your students?

Directions: Listening to students, understanding their needs, and responding to their suggestions are important ways to build relationships in the classroom. Many beginning teachers make the mistake of being a friend to students and then have difficulty being a teacher later in the year. Use the ideas on this page to discuss practical ways to survey your students. Ask your students to complete any of these with short answers. A digital version can be found on the companion website. Share the results with your mentor and what you learned by doing this.

Student Interest Survey

Sample Questions:

- What do you like most about school?
- What do you think your strengths are in the classroom?
- How do you learn best?
- What is your favorite subject? Why?
- What language do you speak at home?
- Have you ever traveled to another country?
- What could I help you learn this year?
- What do you wish you could do in school?
- What is your favorite sport or hobby?
- Do you play a musical instrument?

Adapt questions to meet the needs and ages of students. You may need to read the questions to younger children and write their answers on the board, or students can circle a smiley or frown face to express their opinion.

1. *Option:* Select a question and have students write the answers on an index card. Make sure students write their names on the cards!

2. *Take photographs of each student.* Students love it, and it will help you learn their names and faces. This may be more appropriate for younger students. A whole-class photograph is fun for all age groups.

3. *Interview a few students.* Ask them to talk about their experiences in school and share how they best learn. You can assist your novice teacher in documenting the responses using audio features on phones or tablets. Be sure to get permission from students and parents.

4. *What are your ideas for getting to know your students?*

Companion Website

Creating a Classroom Profile

Key Question: Why is it important to see the entire classroom in one document?

Directions: Complete the information on this chart for all the students in your classroom. Add or delete categories to meet your needs. What do you want to know about your students? Share what you learn about your students with your mentor. A digital version of this form is available on the companion website.

SEPTEMBER

STUDENT Names	Gender	Ethnicity	Age	First Language	Musical Talent	Artistic Interests	Athletic Ability	Learning Style	Special Need

Companion Website

SEPTEMBER

Learning How Students Learn

Key Question: How do you discover your students' learning preferences?

Directions: Being able to recognize the variety of learning styles will assist you in designing effective lessons and engaging students in the learning process.

Think about your preferred teaching style and how it relates to preferred learning styles of your students.

Create a survey or interview your students to find out their learning preferences. Integrate these options into your lesson plans to engage more students. At a mentoring meeting, be prepared to discuss your answers to the questions on this form. A digital version is available on the companion website.

Class Overview of Learning Preferences

I learn best by . . .	List the names of the students in your class who prefer each learning method	
Listening to the teacher, an audio book, or other hearing formats		
Seeing a visual diagram, map, agenda, or other visual formats.		
Using manipulatives, blocks, building models, or other tactile objects.		
Writing essays, paper and pencil, or computer typing		
Writing poetry, songs, or raps		
Singing songs and performing		
Debating, interviewing, and presenting information		
Producing videos		
Reading text in books or on the computer		
Drawing, painting, making diagrams, or making charts		
Using the web to research and find answers		
Acting, dramatization, role playing		
Ask your students to respond to these two prompts	**Names of students**	
1. I prefer to work in groups with other students.		
2. I prefer to learn alone.		

Companion Website

SEPTEMBER

Establishing and Implementing Routines

Key Question: Why is it important to discuss routines with your mentor?

Directions: Routines are important for maintaining consistency and moving through a teaching day in a predictable manner so that students know what to expect. Establishing routines can save valuable time and energy that can be put into academic areas. Discuss these sample routines listed here and review the questions at the end of the page. Create workable routines in your classroom.

1. *Routines at the beginning of the day or beginning of a class*

   - Attendance and how to handle students who are absent so they get make up work

   - Lunch count

   - Collecting homework and recording it

2. *Procedures for students' moving*

   - Walking to classes or in the classroom

   - Leaving during class time to go to the rest room or locker

   - Fire drills and emergency exits

3. *Routines and procedures for academic work*

   - Rewarding good behavior and/or consequences for misbehavior

   - How to listen to others during a discussion

   - What to do when students forget books, pencils, or materials

   - What students do who finish early

4. *Closing of the school day or a class*

   - Collecting work at the end of the day or class

   - Cleaning up materials and supplies

   - Exiting the class or building

Review these questions.

1. What is the purpose of routines and why are they important to classroom management?

2. How will you know when students understand a routine?

3. How does an effective teacher reinforce a routine that is already established?

4. How does an effective teacher introduce a new routine to the class?

5. How do routines save time that can be used for teaching and learning?

Companion Website

Rules, Rewards, and Consequences

Key Question: How do the rules, rewards, and consequences contribute to establishing a positive community of learners?

Directions: Ask your mentor to share the ways rules are created in this school and the types of rules she has in her classroom. Novice teachers who have difficulty managing a classroom often tend to create harsh rules like "no talking!" or "no getting out of your seat," and these *no* rules are problematic for many students who have difficulty if their preferred style of learning is more social. How will you create appropriate rules? Reflect and respond to these questions. E-mail your responses to your mentor and discuss them at your next meeting. Bring a copy of your rules, a sample of rewards, and what consequences you are using.

A digital version can be found on the companion website.

Creating Rules, Rewards, and Consequences That Promote a Positive Learning Environment

1. What rules, rewards, or consequences systems are working for you so far?

2. How do you let students know what the consequences are *prior* to their breaking a rule?

3. What are some problems, issues, or concerns you have about this topic?

4. How is "respect" demonstrated in your classroom? How do you model respect? Refer to the CONNECT page for August to review the respect form on the companion website.

5. What does being a *culturally sensitive teacher* mean to you? How do you demonstrate that?

Learning School Procedures

Key Question: What do you need to know about the following procedures?

Directions: Getting oriented to the systems and policies in a school and district can be frustrating and confusing for a novice teacher. One way you can help is to be proactive and discuss the procedures with your mentor. We all have had experiences of touching a book in the library and finding out there is a *procedure* that this librarian uses. Save yourself from the distress of learning the hard way. Discuss the procedures below with your mentor and find out if there are more school culture issues you need to know about.

1. How does a teacher . . .

   - Sign out books from the resource center or library?

   - Use any computers or other equipment—where to get it and how to sign it out?

   - Reserve books for class lessons?

   - Order paper and school supplies?

   - Deal with medical emergencies?

   - Access student records and special education files?

   - Call for a substitute and leave work for the day?

2. What does a teacher do . . .

   - Before school; and how does she enter the building?

   - During homeroom or lunch room?

   - At recess, bus duty, or study hall?

3. How does a teacher use . . .

   - Faculty-only rooms?

   - The library or computer room?

   - An aide or paraprofessional in the classroom?

Companion Website

Classroom and Behavior Management Issues

Key Question: How do routines minimize disruptions and promote a positive learning environment?

Directions: We all have heard that a prepared and organized teacher has fewer discipline issues in the classroom. To ensure you are prepared means you need to review routines and organizational structures that need to be in place. By discussing these topics with your mentor this month, you minimize the stress that can be created from a disorganized classroom. Review the following topics and select the topics that are most appropriate for you right now.

1. *Classroom Routines and Organization*

   - Review what you are doing in your classroom to organize your space, time, and materials. Invite your mentor to visit and share your procedures.

   - Ask your mentor to share effective systems for correcting papers, organizing materials, and grading student work. Ask him to share routines that save time and that may have taken years for him to figure out. Use the systems that fit for you.

   - Organize a *sharing* meeting and invite other novice teachers to meet with you to share successful ideas for organizing systems that save time in the classroom.

   - Ask your mentor to share efficient ways to begin and end lessons so that housekeeping activities required (such as collecting lunch money or homework) take minimal time away from classroom instruction.

2. *Behavior Issues With Individual Students or the Whole Class*

   - List any problems you are having with specific students right now. Share the problems with your mentor or other beginning teachers in your support group to gather possible ideas.

   - Schedule time to interview teachers at the school who have creative ways to avoid behavior problems. Ask your mentor to give you names of teachers they have observed as successful.

   - Discuss appropriate consequences for situations that arise in the classroom with your mentor. Share the difference between students not completing homework and students who are seriously disrespectful to others and why the consequences have to be different.

Looking at Student Work Together

Key Question: How can looking at student work samples help you improve your teaching practice?

Directions: Bring a set of completed student assignments to a meeting with your mentor. Select three students from the class randomly (without looking at names). If you are using a school-based rubric for assessing student work, use that to review the assignment and grade each student. Ask your mentor to also do this process. Compare and share your assessments of the students. Are they close? Why would they be different?

1. Decide on the criteria for assessment and then rate the three random papers separately using the school rubric or use this one. You and the mentor will use the same three papers for this activity.

1	2	3	4	5
Does not meet any criteria	Meets a few criteria	Meets some criteria	Meets most criteria	Meets all criteria

2. Compare and share how you rated the students with your mentor. Discuss any differences in ratings and explain why you rated a student that way.

3. What is difficult about rating student work?

4. Why is this important to review student work with each other each month?

Companion Website

Communicating With Parents

Key Question: Why is it important to communicate with parents regularly?

Directions: Discuss ways you could communicate with parents this month. Review the examples here and add your own.

1. **Examples of communication may include the following:**

   - *A letter mailed to the home.* Ask your mentor to share samples of letters that have been sent to parents from teachers in the school. If the school sends a formal letter welcoming students, review that letter with your mentor. Will you also write a letter to students?

   - *A letter sent via the students.* It may be easier to write a letter and give it to the students to hand deliver to the parents sometime during the first week of school. Ask your mentor if this is a good idea. Some teachers may want to have a return receipt to ensure the parents or guardians received the communication.

   - *An e-mail to parents.* Some school systems have parent communication through e-mail. If this is an option at your school, discuss the appropriate ways to do this. The down side for e-mail is that the parents then have access to you 24 hours a day, and this may be overwhelming.

   - *Letters or e-mails could include a brief biography of who you are, some examples of what the curriculum will include this year, and ways the parents can keep in touch. Policies for homework and expectations for materials students should bring to class may also be included.*

2. **Organize a classroom social**

If the school does not sponsor an official Open House, you may ask your mentor to help you organize a social to meet and greet the parents. It could be a "coffee and conversation" early in the morning before students arrive or an early evening after parents leave work. The goal is to have parents meet you early in the year, so if you need to be in touch later, they already know who you are and your classroom procedures.

3. **Why it is important to connect with parents early**

   - Builds a relationship with the teacher before there are any student behavior issues.

   - Demonstrates that the teacher is reaching out to share what is going on in the classroom.

   - Allows the teacher to share expectations for learning and homework and gain support.

   - Allows teachers, based on the response from parents, to get an indication of who is willing and able to connect—for example, those parents who may not speak English or parents who work night shifts and cannot attend meetings. This gives you the time to create alternative ways to communicate throughout the school year. It also lets you know the parents who cannot attend scheduled conferences but who do still care about their children's progress.

Companion Website

September Novice Teacher Reflections

Directions: Complete any of these prompts to summarize your experience this month, or add your own. Compare and share your reflections with your mentor or other novice teachers in your support group. You can also complete these reflections in your Novice Teacher Journal.

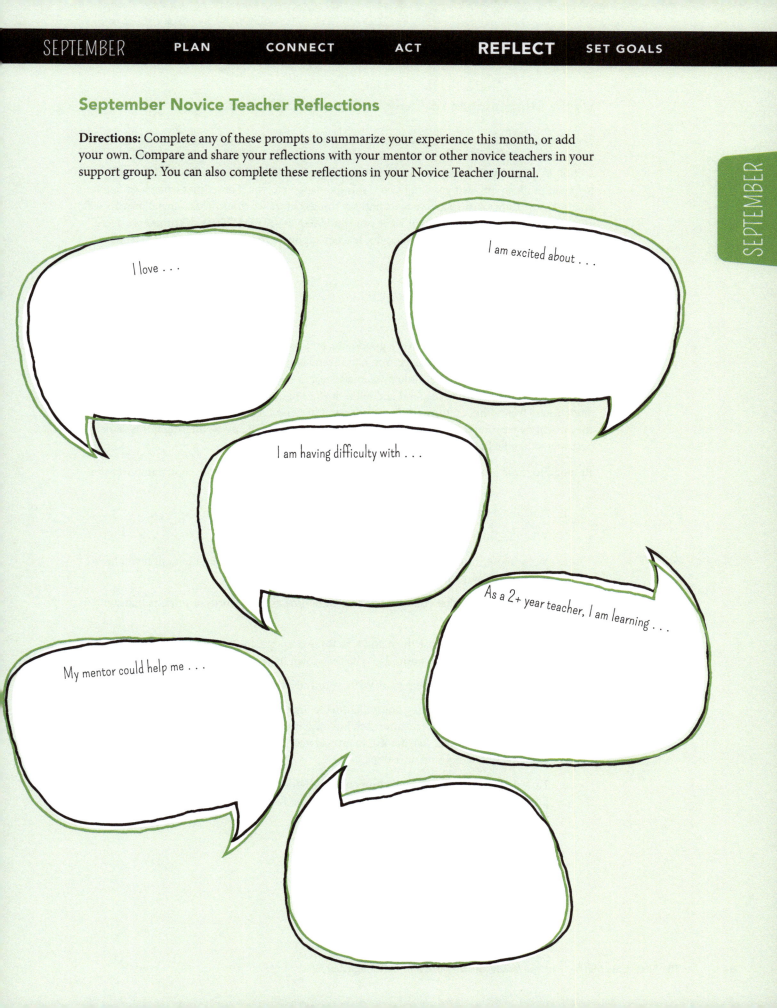

I love . . .

I am excited about . . .

I am having difficulty with . . .

As a 2+ year teacher, I am learning . . .

My mentor could help me . . .

Using Mindfulness to Explore Teaching Dilemmas

Teaching is complex, and often there are not clear answers to situations that arise while you are being mentored. The teaching dilemmas introduced at the end of each month in the REFLECT section may not always apply to you; however, the process of reflecting on this dilemma will help you think about what you might do if this did happen to you. Sometimes when a situation arises that we didn't anticipate, we react and say things before we think. This journal process will allow you to pause and think about what you would like to say next. These dilemmas are useful for mentoring conversation starters, novice teacher support group discussions, and personal reflection.

Dilemma 2: Including All Students in the Community of Learners

You are beginning the school year on a good note, and your mentor has visited your classroom to see how you are organizing the space. You had several behavior problems this month, so you had to separate the most disruptive students from the rest of the class. Your mentor asked about this, and you didn't know how to respond and felt that you might be doing something wrong. These students are from other cultures, and you wonder if because English is not their first language, they might be frustrated. Now that your mentor has seen this, you are wondering if this is the best way to handle their behavior. *What do you do?*

Respond to these prompts in your Novice Teacher Journal, available on the companion website.

1. State the dilemma as clearly as possible in one sentence if you can.

2. What decision do you need to make in regard to this situation?

3. Write about the emotions that come up for you that relate to this situation. If you have two choices, write how the emotions might be different.

4. Stop and reread what you have written. Underline any key words or phrases that stand out for you.

5. Soften your eyes or close them and take three deep breaths. Ask yourself, what am I missing that I have not noticed? Write that down in your journal.

6. How can your mentor help you? Write your reflection in your journal.

7. If you are truly stuck, bring your dilemma to another novice teacher who is in their second or third year of teaching. Ask him or her to listen and to ask you questions to clarify your dilemma. Ask her not to give advice, just to ask you questions to help you clarify your feelings and next steps.

8. How do you feel about this dilemma now? All dilemmas are not resolved! This is a process of clarifying and understanding how you feel and how you might proceed in the future.

Directions: Complete the goal-setting processes alone or with your mentor. Write your responses on this page or in your Novice Teacher Journal, available on the companion website.

1. *Goal for Improving Your Teaching Practices*

   - Review the PLAN–CONNECT–ACT–REFLECT pages you completed in this chapter with your mentor. Look ahead to October ACTs to see what you may focus on to continue development.

   - Acknowledge what you are learning! Be specific about what you have done that is working.

   - Reflect on your teaching this month. What will you do differently next month?

   - Agree on ONE goal with your mentor to reinforce your learning for next month.

   - Goal:

2. *Goal to Support Your Social and Emotional Well-Being*

   - Discuss any challenges you may be facing right now. Challenges often bring stress.

   - Don't ignore any signs of stress! Pay attention and ask your mentor about ways to manage stress.

   - Continue to learn about mindfulness by reading "Five Simple Lessons for Social and Emotional Learning for Adults," available on the companion website.

   - Goal:

"

A good teacher walks around the classroom helping everyone do things they don't understand.
—SEVENTH-GRADE STUDENT

NOVICE TEACHER PHASE: OVERWHELMED

"There is so much to do in one day!"

NOVICE TEACHER AFFIRMATION

I am inspired to be the best teacher I can be.

OCTOBER

TEACHING FOR UNDERSTANDING
Planning and Delivering Effective Instruction

GUIDING QUESTIONS

1. How do you design effective lesson and unit plans? The **Planning ACTivities** will provide ways to approach this task.

2. How will you include students in your mentoring conversations? Use the **Student ACTivities** as a way to focus on student voices and work.

3. Why is it important to reach out to parents? Use the **Communication ACTivity** as a way to focus on ways to connect with parents and families.

Interstate Teacher Assessment and Support Consortium—InTASC Standards

Review InTASC Standards 4 and 7 with your mentor.

- **Standard 4 Content**

The teacher understands the central concepts, tools of inquiry, and structures of the discipline(s) he or she teaches and creates learning experiences that make these aspects of the discipline accessible and meaningful for learners to ensure mastery of the content.

- **Standard 7 Planning for Instruction**

The teacher plans instruction that supports every student in meeting rigorous learning goals by drawing upon knowledge of content areas, curriculum, cross-disciplinary skills, and pedagogy, as well as knowledge of learners and the community context.

Chapter Overview

Getting through the first two months of school for any beginning teacher takes energy and lots of support. You may be overwhelmed by the amount of work you need to accomplish in any given day, and you may be afraid to share that thought with anyone in the school. "What will my mentor think of me?" may cross your mind. Be gentle with yourself and don't compare yourself with your mentor.

At this time of year, you may be questioning, what are my students expected to know and be able to do? How can I understand the curriculum in a way that I can teach it effectively? Ask questions. Use the ACTivities pages to uncover what you already know about teaching and focus on the topics that you will find most useful this month.

What kind of expertise or life skills do you bring to the classroom? How can you use them in the classes you are teaching? Do you have computer skills? Share your current ideas and skills with your mentor and other teachers in the school. They will love it! Most teachers are lifelong learners and want to pick up new skills. Don't be shy.

You will notice that Classroom and Behavior Management, Looking at Student Work, and Communicating With Parents sections are in every chapter. If you have a particular need to read all the Classroom and Behavior Management topics now, do it! Then you can review the topics again each month. These discussions are ongoing throughout your professional life and will not be learned or mastered in one month.

Every effective teacher will tell you that lesson planning is critical success. The way a teacher plans influences her ability to organize and structure her time in the classroom. It also minimizes classroom disruption and lets the novice teacher have a clear outline for what will be done in a class or over a time frame if it is a unit of study. How will you talk about lesson planning with your mentor? Use this month to talk about teaching expectations and curriculum requirements too.

If you are in a novice teacher support group, ask other teachers to share what they are doing to create community in their classrooms. Novice teachers feel less overwhelmed when they are talking with other beginners who are facing the same issues.

Your Novice Teacher Affirmation this month is, "I am inspired to be the best teacher I can be." Don't lose your positive attitude. It does get easier as you move through the year. Ask your mentor what helps her to stay inspired. Focus on the quote from the student this month and walk around the room helping them to learn.

Follow the PLAN, CONNECT, ACT, REFLECT and SET GOALS sections in this chapter to guide your mentoring conversations and reflections. Watch and listen to a mentor share her insights in Video 2.7, *Mentoring in Action: October Chapter Introduction*, on the companion website or scan the QR code on a mobile device.

Watch Video 2.8, *Advice for New Teachers From Other Beginning Teachers*, available on the companion website or scan the QR code on a mobile device. Share what you learned with your mentor.

VIDEO 2.7

Mentoring in Action: October Chapter Introduction

VIDEO 2.8

Advice for New Teachers From Other Beginning Teachers

OCTOBER

Novice Teacher Journal

One way to plan your month is to assess where you are right now. Writing in your Novice Teacher Journal will help you document what you are feeling and how to focus your teaching. A digital version of the journal is available on the companion website.

Directions: Review the chapter cover page and the overview for this month. How do this month's topic, the quotes, phase, and affirmation relate to you right now? How are you feeling this month? What do you feel confident about? Where do you need some help?

Use your journal to record your thoughts, feelings, and questions in a free-flowing narrative. This page is for your personal reflection; it does not need to be shared with your mentor unless you choose to do so. At the end of the year, you can review your monthly reflections to see how much you have grown.

October Entry Date_____

Today I feel . . .

_____

_____

_____

I am confident in the areas of . . .

_____

_____

_____

I need some help . . .

_____

_____

_____

Questions for Participating in Mentoring Conversations

Sometimes you don't know what to ask your mentor because you don't know what you don't know! Review this list and choose some questions that are useful to you. How will your mentor respond? Will you schedule a face-to-face meeting, a phone appointment, or send an e-mail? What works best for both of you? Reflect on your mentor's responses and think about what works for you. If you are a 2+ year teacher, these may not all apply to you; however, there may be a question you would like to revisit.

Your Possible Questions

1. What does the district expect of me as a first-year (or 2+ years) teacher?

2. How can I learn the district curriculum and goals?

3. How do I make content meaningful when I have the test scores as outcomes of success?

4. How much planning do I have to do? Are my plans reviewed by the principal?

5. Will I be observed this month?

6. How can I "backward" plan so I can get through the content in a timely way?

7. Can you give me some successful strategies for engaging learners in interactive ways that won't lead to misbehavior?

Other questions I have . . .

Anticipate Your Mentor's Questions

1. What do you know about teaching for understanding? Have you taken a course that covers this topic?

2. What do you already know about our district goals and curriculum?

3. How do you like teachers to make content meaningful for you as a student?

4. What can I do to assist you right now that would reduce your anxiety?

Meetings and Observations

Plan brief weekly meetings with your mentor. The ACTs in this chapter serve as mentoring conversation starters and can also be used to assess or review what you may already know about a given topic.

Plan to meet at times that allow you to have quality time together in a place without interruptions. Knowing when you will meet each week reduces anxiety for you. You will find that you look forward to regularly scheduled meetings especially if they are short. Use this calendar to document your meetings and invite your mentor to schedule classroom visits to see you in action. There are many videos in this book and also in your mentor's *Mentoring in Action* book. Consider scheduling time to watch the videos together and have a discussion. A digital version of this calendar (October Calendar.pdf) is available on the companion website.

If you have not invited your mentor to visit your classroom yet, do it this month. She can help you more by seeing your space. Explain why things are in certain places and why you have developed your routines.

October Calendar

MONDAY	TUESDAY	WEDNESDAY	THURSDAY	FRIDAY

Use this calendar to PLAN the month with your mentor as well as to document meetings.

OCTOBER

CONNECT to Additional Resources

CONNECT to School and District Resources

What resources exist in your school and community that could assist you in October?

CONNECT With Colleagues, Parents, and Families

What are the protocols for communicating with parents and families? Ask your mentor.

CONNECT to Student Voices

Watch the *Teachers Make a Difference* video, available on the companion website, with your mentor to hear a candid statement from a high school student. Respond to these prompts and compare your answers. What surprised you in what Jennifer shared? How does Jennifer's perspective influence your thinking about teaching and learning?

CONNECT to Education Hot Topics

Include the Arts! Creativity and the arts can get lost in the classroom when the focus is often on test scores and achievement. Review the articles on *Teach HUB Magazine* online to find some ideas for integrating creativity into everyday school assignments. By giving students options for demonstrating their learning, you will be engaging more learners.

CONNECT With the Companion Website

Video links, forms for this chapter, a featured book and other resources by the author are located at resources.corwin.com/mentoringinaction

OCTOBER

The First ACT!

Differentiating Mentoring Conversations

Teaching is complex work, and you can easily become overwhelmed. It is appropriate to customize your mentoring conversations so that your mentor is responding to your needs and skills.

Directions: Discuss the prompts with your mentor or think about them on your own. Refer to your state or district teaching standards to note a common language for teaching and summarize your key ideas in each box. Skim the ACTS for this month and decide which topics are most relevant to your needs this month.

Name_____ Date _____

Monthly Needs Assessment

1. What is going well in your classroom right now?	3. What would you like to improve or enhance in your practice this month?
2. How do you know your practice is working? What is your evidence of success?	4. Review the ACT overview of possible conversations for this month with your mentor. What would you like to focus on this month?

A digital version of this template (Monthly Needs Assessment Sample With Standards.pdf) is available on the companion website. Keep a copy of this assessment in your professional file.

Companion Website

Overview of the ACTs for October Conversations

Directions: Skim the ACTivities listed here and complete the pages that will forward your learning. If you are a 2+ year teacher, revisit any ACTs you already completed or try some new ACTs to stretch your thinking. Digital copies of some of the ACTs are available on the companion website.

Key Question Topic	ACTivities	PAGE
Planning	ACT 1 **Organizing a Lesson Plan**	75
Planning	ACT 2 **Questions About Planning**	76
Planning	ACT 3 **Planning for Understanding**	77
Planning	ACT 4 **Engaging Learners**	78
Planning	ACT 5 **Pacing a Lesson**	79
Planning	ACT 6 **Unit Planning**	80
Students	ACT 7 **Student Perspectives**	81
Students	ACT 8 **Classroom and Behavior Management Issues**	82
Students	ACT 9 **Looking at Student Work Together**	83
Communication	ACT 10 **Communicating With Parents**	84

Organizing a Lesson Plan

Key Question: How will you review lesson plan formats with your mentor?

Directions: Review this sample format for a lesson plan and the questions in each section. If your district requires a different format, find out from your mentor now. Ask about ways to use a long form plan and a shorter version for the plan book. Ask your mentor to share his planning process.

Sample Planning Template

Lesson Plan Title: *Write the name of the topic or class here*   **Date:** *Day you teach lesson*

Time of Class: *Period or time*   **Length of period:** *How much time to teach*

Subject: *Content*

Purpose of Lesson: *Why are you teaching this lesson?*

State Standard: *What is the standard you are reaching?*

Objective: *Bloom's taxonomy verb—what the student will achieve or accomplish*

Theme or Unit Number ___: *Is this an isolated lesson or part of a bigger curriculum unit?*

Key Questions: *The questions you will introduce to the students to guide the discussion and activities of the lesson should be broadly designed to encourage discussion and critical thinking.*

Procedure: *Note that the class period includes other housekeeping activities, such as collecting papers, announcing future school activities, or collecting lunch money. These need to be incorporated into the lesson plan to avoid running out of teaching time.*

Closing the Lesson: *How will you know students learned? Is there a summary? Will you use any informal assessments here?*

Homework: *Required or enrichment?*

Revise this template to meet your needs.

OCTOBER

Questions About Planning

Key Question: What do you need to know about planning?

Directions: Co-plan a lesson with your mentor using the following questions to guide your discussion.

1. *Why am I teaching this lesson?* required curriculum? student interest? novice teacher interest? other?

2. *What do I hope to accomplish?* skill development? concept to be discussed for understanding? product to be produced?

3. *Who are the students?* range of abilities? range of ages? ethnic diversity and varying cultures?

4. *What is the time frame for teaching this lesson?* part of a unit? one period or block schedule? isolated lesson?

5. *How will I begin the lesson to capture student attention?* story, anecdote? relevance to their lives? props or visual displays?

6. *Will I need other resources to teach this lesson?* audiovisual or technology? student handouts? manipulatives or visual displays?

7. *How will students spend their time during the lesson?* small-group discussion? individual? large group? hands-on activity or experiment? taking notes or observing?

8. *How will the learning in this lesson be assessed?* formal? quiz or test? informal? observation of learning? open-ended questions? written? verbal?

9. *How will I summarize the lesson and close the class period?* review and summary? collecting papers? giving next assignment? allowing time for homework or questions?

10. *Will there be homework or enrichment activities offered?* how will I collect later? is it required or extra? will it count? what is a cooperating teacher's policy? how will I grade it?

11. *How will I know whether I succeeded in teaching the lesson?* self-assessment? response of students? cooperating teacher input?

12. *How will the next lesson relate to or build on this one?*

Planning for Understanding

Key Question: Why do you need to understand how planning relates to student learning?

Directions: An effective lesson plan promotes student learning and skill development. Discuss with your mentor what students should know, understand, and be able to do *as a result of teaching a lesson.*

Four Steps to Effective Lesson Planning

1. *Think about breadth or depth* as you design your lessons and units.

    Are you aiming for breadth in your lessons (e.g., being able to connect this concept to other concepts or relevant experiences)?

    *   Students explain why or why not.
    *   Students extend the concept to others.
    *   Students think about and give examples of similar concepts.

    Are you aiming for depth in your lessons (i.e., looking more at the detail about this idea)?

    *   Students question the information.
    *   Students analyze the facts.
    *   Students prove something.

2. *Set priorities* for assessing student growth in lessons and units.

    What do you expect all students to be familiar with?

    *   To be able to do in this class?
    *   To really understand for lasting learning?

3. *Select measurement tools* to determine student understanding.

    How will you know students understand what you are teaching?

    *   What do *all* students have to know? How will you know?
    *   What do *most* students have to know? How will you know?
    *   What will *some* students have to know? How will you know?

4. *Create meaningful learning experiences* that engage and support learning (not just busy work).

    *   Have you included a hook to gain attention and provide relevance?
    *   Do you have key questions that promote discussion and thinking?
    *   Do you have time for students to practice and engage in activity?
    *   Do you allow students time to reflect on their work and set goals?

Engaging Learners

Key Question: What strategies will help you engage learners throughout the length of a class?

Directions: Engaging learners when they are transitioning from the hallway to a classroom can be challenging. Beginning the class with a reading, a prop, or a demonstration creates curiosity and a focus on the teacher. Higher order thinking also engages learners because their responses take more time, and they need to think about them. Bloom's Taxonomy is one way to integrate language into the lesson plan. Review the chart with your mentor and discuss ways to engage through these activities.

Level of Understanding	Example Verbs
6 Evaluation	choose, conclude, evaluate, defend, rank, support, rate
5 Synthesis	construct, create, formulate, revise, write, plan, predict
4 Analysis	analyze, classify, compare, contrast, debate, categorize
3 Application	apply, demonstrate, draw, show, solve, illustrate
2 Comprehension	describe, explain, paraphrase, summarize, rewrite
1 Knowledge	define, identify, label, list, memorize, spell, name

Companion Website

Pacing a Lesson

Key Question: How will you structure teaching time effectively?

Directions: One of the biggest concerns teachers have about teaching is that they don't have enough time in the day to do all there is to do. The majority of the time spent in class should be on teaching the curriculum, not on making announcements, collecting lunch money, passing out materials, getting students into groups, or cleaning up. However, these tasks do need to get done too.

A class period is your *allocated teaching time*, but it also needs to include housekeeping activities. *Instructional time* is the time when students are actually engaged in learning activities. A lesson plan is the way to organize a teacher's time to ensure the focus is on teaching and learning.

Use the time chart below with one of your lesson plans and put in the number of minutes that should be allotted to complete each section of the plan. Share your results with your mentor. Do you need to make any adjustments in your pacing?

Allocated Class Time: How much should you spend?		
How much time? 5%	Starting Class Period Housekeeping Activities	• Required tasks • Collection of homework
10%	BEGINNING LESSON Introducing or connecting to previous day Introducing objectives, vocabulary, and key questions	• Motivation/relevance • Overview • Directions • Purpose of lesson
70%	MIDDLE Facilitating a variety of activities for student learning	• Objective • Key questions • Students engaged in learning • Activity • Knowledge • Student sharing • Informal assessment and checking for understanding
10%	CLOSING Summarizing and reviewing lesson Setting goals for next lesson	• Wrap up • Review of key points • Collection of materials/papers
5%	Ending Class Period Housekeeping Activities	• Required tasks • Collection of class work

Companion Website

Unit Planning

Key Question: How will you develop effective unit plans?

A unit is an organized group of lesson plans with a beginning, various activities, and a culmination activity. The unit may be subject based, interdisciplinary, or thematic. It can last as long as a semester or as short as a week. It has overarching themes and concepts to be learned through daily lessons. A unit will have a general outline or plan for implementation and the daily lesson plans that demonstrate in detail how the plan is to be carried out in the classroom. Lesson plans are part of the unit and would follow the format required.

Directions: Teachers typically organize their teaching in units by skills for early childhood, by subjects or themes for elementary/middle level, or by subject area topics at secondary levels. Units are organized around books students have read, historical events, science themes, topics, or state testing topics. Discuss how your school organizes units of study with your mentor. Review these overarching questions together.

Questions to Review With Your Mentor

- What is the purpose of the unit?

- How much time is allotted to complete the unit? How many lessons?

- What do students already know about this topic?

- What would students like to learn or know?

- How will the unit be introduced?

- What are the key questions that need to be answered?

- Is prior knowledge necessary?

- Will the unit have a theme?

- Will the unit cross disciplines? Is team teaching involved?

- Will any special activities be part of the unit?

- Will I need special materials or audiovisual for this unit?

- Will guest speakers or field trips be part of the unit?

- Other questions you may introduce . . .

Companion Website

OCTOBER

Student Perspectives

Key Question: Why do student perspectives matter?

Planning and delivering effective instruction requires the students be full participants in their learning. Novice teachers often struggle because they know their content but say the students just won't listen. Planning effective lessons certainly is important, but clearly the students have a lot to say about how they learn best.

In Part I, an interactive PDF titled "Integrating Student Perspectives Into Mentoring Conversations" is highlighted as a way to talk about students. This resource includes sample student surveys, a protocol for the mentor, and videos of mentoring conversations that illustrate how to talk about student survey data with your mentor.

Directions: Watch Video 2.9, *Reactions to the Student Survey*, with your mentor and discuss why it is important to ask the students what they think. Review the sample surveys available in the *Using Student Perspectives Interactive Guide* PDF located in Part I on the companion website and create a survey with your mentor. Review these questions to guide your discussion.

Creating an Anonymous Student Survey

1. What was your reaction to the video?

2. What do you want to know from your students to improve your teaching?

3. Which questions on the sample survey can you use?

4. What new questions will you add?

5. How will you and your mentor administer the survey?

6. When will you review the data?

Before meeting with your mentor to discuss the survey results, watch Video 2.10, *Using a Seven Step Protocol to Discuss Student Survey Data With Novice Teachers,* so you know what to expect in the mentoring conversation when it relates to data. Review sample conversations on the companion website and select the grade level that is closest to yours or watch them all!

VIDEO 2.9

Reactions to the Student Survey

VIDEO 2.10

Using a Seven Step Protocol to Discuss Student Survey Data With Novice Teachers

Companion Website

Classroom and Behavior Management Issues

Key Question: What do you need to think about before disciplining a student?

Directions: Review these questions with your mentor so that you understand what they mean. Keep this list near if you need to use it. Before reacting, think about what the best way to approach this student would be.

1. Who is the student?

   Does this student have a prearranged plan when disruptive? For example, is the student sent to guidance, principal, or resource or learning center classroom?

   Is this a first offense, or is this repeated misbehavior? Is this common misbehavior for others?

   Does this student have a special need that has not been addressed?

   Are there other adults who need to be notified when this student is disruptive?

2. What rule did the student break?

   Is it a major offense? for example, hitting someone or possessing a weapon.

   Is it a minor offense? for example, chewing gum or wearing a hat.

   Is it related to academic work? for example, not doing homework or cheating.

   Is it related to work habits? for example, not listening in class.

   What did the student specifically do or say?

   Is this misbehavior appropriate for the student's age?

3. Where did the misbehavior take place?

   In classroom?

   On playground, hallway, cafeteria, en route to class?

   Off school grounds but near school?

4. Do you have personal feelings about this student?

   Have you interacted positively or negatively before this?

   Do you know this student at all?

5. What are your legal rights when dealing with disruptive students?

   State and local guidelines for restraining students, searching lockers, or other?

   School policies related to alcohol, drugs, weapons?

   Students with educational plans?

Looking at Student Work Together

Key Question: How can looking at student work samples assist you in being a more effective teacher?

Directions: Bring several samples from one lesson to a meeting with your mentor. Review the samples with these lenses: standards, quality, and expectations. Ask your mentor why is it so important to discuss looking at student work systematically.

Three Lenses for Looking at Work

1. *Standards*

   What was the objective of this assignment? Is that clear in the samples?

   What were the students supposed to accomplish? Did they?

2. *Quality*

   What did the work look like? Is it presented neatly?

   Can you tell if the students are proud of their work?

3. *Expectations*

   What did the novice teacher expect the student(s) to do on this assignment?

   Are those expectations limiting the student's achievement?

Companion Website

Communicating With Parents

Key Question: Why is it important to tell parents what is going on in school?

Directions: Parents often ask their children, "What did you do in school today?" Students respond, "Nothing!" We all know that is not true. Often, communication from the teacher comes when there is a problem; and then parents are on the defensive. Reflect on these ideas and discuss positive ways to connect with parents with your mentor.

Newsletters

Why not put the students to work and have them write short articles about the lessons they are learning in school and turn it into a newsletter for parents? Novice teachers can use this as a learning experience for students while informing parents. *Education Matters!* could be the name of the newsletter, or students could vote on a name they like. Students can hand deliver the newsletter, or it could be mailed or e-mailed directly to the parents.

Classroom Open House

Another way novice teachers can connect with parents and share what is going in the classroom is to host an open house in the classroom. Invite the parents in for "coffee and conversation" early in the morning before students arrive or include students. Share the logistics of this type of event with your mentor. Brainstorm ways students can show off their work and how you can let parents know how they can help their children learn.

Classroom Web Page

Many teachers entering the profession have technology skills and are able to create web pages. If your school and district have the capabilities for a web-based newsletter, encourage the novice teachers to do it. It is a fun and easy way to get the parents' attention!

Cable TV Show

Another option for sharing what is going on could be a classroom TV show. Let students produce and direct a show that lets parents know what they are learning. Novice teachers may not have time for one on their own, but perhaps several teachers could get together and put on short segments. It would also be a great way to introduce the novice teachers to the school district!

October Novice Teacher Reflections

Directions: Complete any of these prompts to summarize your experience this month, or add your own. Compare and share your reflections with your mentor or other novice teachers in your support group. You can also complete these prompts in your Novice Teacher Journal.

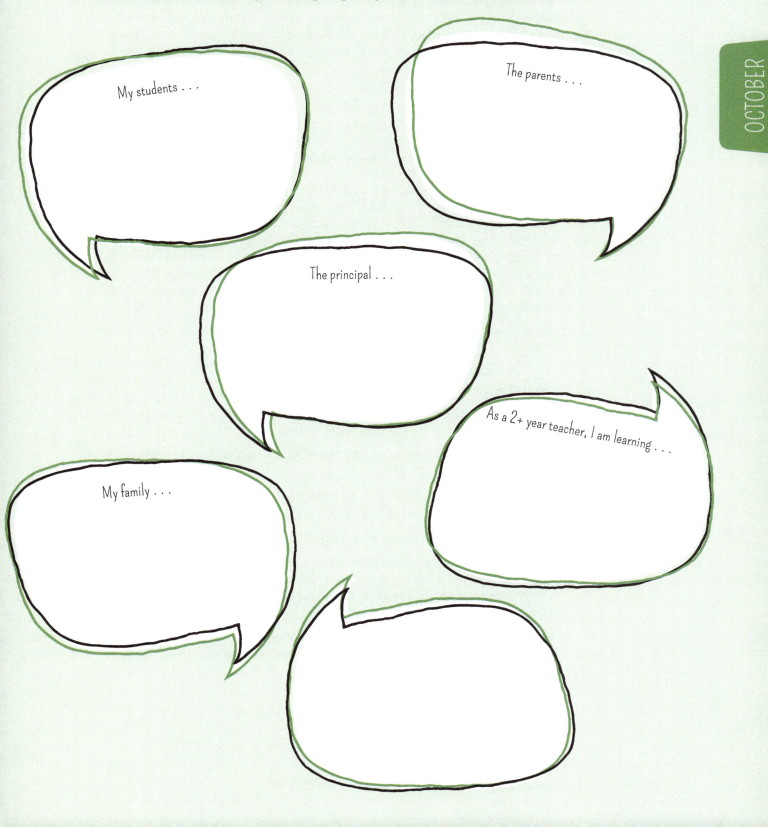

My students . . .

The parents . . .

The principal . . .

As a 2+ year teacher, I am learning . . .

My family . . .

Using Mindfulness to Explore Teaching Dilemmas

Teaching is complex, and often there are not clear answers to situations that arise while you are being mentored. The teaching dilemmas introduced at the end of each month in the REFLECT section may not always apply to you; however, the process of reflecting on this dilemma will help you think about what you might do if this did happen to you. Sometimes when a situation arises that we didn't anticipate, we react and say things before we think. This journal process will allow you to pause and think about what you would like to say next. These dilemmas are useful for mentoring conversation starters, novice teacher support group discussions, and personal reflection.

Dilemma 3: Overwhelmed With So Many Suggestions From Your Mentor

Your mentor decides to pop in for an unannounced short observation (which you agreed she could do any time) and watch the opening of a lesson. You are having a bad day and several of your teaching practices are not working. Your mentor has given you many ideas, but you are finding it difficult to implement them all. Students are not paying attention, and you forgot to do your lesson plan last night so you are "winging" your lesson. You have shared in your meetings with your mentor that you understand the importance of planning, but when you have to actually do it, you struggle with finding the time. You are already working late every night correcting papers, and sometimes the planning gets missed. Now, you get so frustrated that you shout, "Heads down" just to get a moment to gain control. Your mentor had given you some strategies, but they just didn't work. She is now leaving and says you will talk later. *What do you do?*

Respond to these prompts in your Novice Teacher Journal, available on the companion website.

1. State the dilemma as clearly as possible in one sentence if you can.

2. What decision do you need to make in regard to this situation?

3. Write about the emotions that come up for you that relate to this situation. If you have two choices, write how the emotions might be different.

4. Stop and reread what you have written. Underline any key words or phrases that stand out for you.

5. Soften your eyes or close them and take three deep breaths. Ask yourself, what am I missing that I have not noticed. Write that down in your journal.

6. How can your mentor help you? Write your reflection in your journal.

7. If you are truly stuck, bring your dilemma to another novice teacher who is in their second or third year of teaching. Ask him or her to listen and to ask you questions to clarify your dilemma. Ask her not to give advice, just to ask you questions to help you clarify your feelings and next steps.

8. How do you feel about this dilemma now? All dilemmas are not resolved! This is a process of clarifying and understanding how you feel and how you might proceed in the future.

Directions: Complete the goal-setting processes alone or with your mentor. Write your responses on this page or in your Novice Teacher Journal, available on the companion website.

1. *Goal for Improving Your Teaching Practices*

   - Review the PLAN–CONNECT–ACT–REFLECT pages you completed in this chapter with your mentor. Look ahead to November ACTs to see what you may focus on to continue development.

   - Acknowledge what you are learning. Invite your mentor to visit your classroom and share.

   - Reflect on your teaching this month. What stands out as effective? What will you do differently next month?

   - Agree on ONE goal with your mentor to reinforce your learning for next month.

   - Goal:

2. *Goal to Support Your Social and Emotional Well-Being*

   - Discuss any challenges you may be facing right now. Challenges often bring stress.

   - Don't ignore any signs of stress! Pay attention and learn ways to manage stress.

   - Continue to learn about mindfulness by watching Kelly McGonigle's TED Talks, *How to Make Stress Your Friend.*

   - Goal:

> **"** I know I have learned something when I have the confidence to do it alone.
>
> —FOURTH-GRADE STUDENT

NOVICE TEACHER PHASE: DISILLUSIONED

"I'm not sure if I made the right choice to teach. This is really hard."

NOVICE TEACHER AFFIRMATION

My ability to listen to student perspectives has the potential to transform my teaching practices.

ASSESSING DIVERSE LEARNERS

*How Do Teachers Know
Students Have Learned?*

GUIDING QUESTIONS

1. How do you plan lessons with assessment in mind? The **Planning ACTivities** will provide ways to think about integrating assessment into lesson plans.

2. How will you learn about assessment tools? The **Tools ACTivities** offer you ideas to discuss.

3. How will you use student perspectives and voice? Use the **Student ACTivities** as a way to guide your conversations.

4. What is important to review regarding parents this month? Use the **Communication ACTivity** as a way to focus.

~~~~~~

Interstate Teacher Assessment and Support Consortium—InTASC Standards

Review InTASC Standard 6.

- **Standard 6 Assessment**

The teacher understands and uses multiple methods of assessment to engage learners in their own growth, to monitor learner progress, and to guide the teacher's and learner's decision making.

~~~~~~

Chapter Overview

Confidence and competence are important feelings for a beginning teacher, and you may not feel either of these right now. In fact at this time of year, you may feel overwhelmed and disillusioned, wondering why and how you got into this career. Turn to your mentor and other teachers for support if you are feeling this way. This is a normal phase of teaching! We all went through it the first year. In fact, many veteran teachers are disillusioned every November!

Review the fourth-grade student's quote on the first page of this chapter, "I know I have learned something when I have the confidence to do it alone." In some ways, this is you. As you become comfortable with the content you are required to teach, you gain more confidence in yourself as a teacher. You are a learner this year, just like your own students. Ask yourself how much your students are learning so far this year. Then ask yourself how much you are learning about how to teach students how to learn.

Review all the pages for November to see what your focus will be. Write in the book or place sticky notes on important pages. Highlight key phrases. This is your journey. You will want to have this book as a resource for next year, so make it your own.

Follow the PLAN, CONNECT, ACT, REFLECT, and SET GOALS sections in this chapter to guide your mentoring conversations and reflections. Use the ACTivities in this chapter to discuss important ways to tap into students' prior knowledge and monitor their progress. Ask your mentor how he does this. Learning styles of students will affect the assessments you use to measure growth. What is your role as a teacher in learning how to assess diverse learners? Remember, you have your own learning style and teaching style, and these may be different from your students'!

Watch and listen to a mentor share her insights in Video 2.11, *Mentoring in Action: November Chapter Introduction*, on the companion website or scan the QR code on a mobile device.

VIDEO 2.11

Mentoring in Action: November Chapter Introduction

Novice Teacher Journal

One way to plan your month is to assess where you are right now. Writing in your Novice Teacher Journal will help you document what you are feeling and how to focus your teaching. A digital version of the journal is available on the companion website.

Directions: Review the chapter cover page and the overview for this month. How do this month's topic, the quotes, phase, and affirmation relate to you right now? How are you feeling as you prepare for the school year to begin? What do you feel confident about? Where do you need some help?

Use your journal to record your thoughts, feelings, and questions in a free-flowing narrative. This page is for your personal reflection; it does not need to be shared with your mentor unless you choose to do so. At the end of the year, you can review your monthly reflections to see how much you have grown.

November Entry Date_____

Today I feel . . .

_____

_____

_____

I am confident in the areas of . . .

_____

_____

_____

I need some help . . .

_____

_____

_____

Companion Website

Questions for Participating in Mentoring Conversations

Sometimes you don't know what to ask your mentor because you don't know what you don't know! Review this list and choose some questions that are useful to you. How will your mentor respond? Will you schedule a face-to-face meeting, or a phone appointment, or send an e-mail? What works best for both of you? Reflect on your mentor's responses and think about what works for you. If you are a 2+ year teacher, these may not all apply to you; however, there may be a question you would like to revisit.

Your Possible Questions

1. Who are my students (languages, learning styles, special needs, learning modifications, family background, etc.)?

2. What do I need to know about their parents that will assist me?

3. How can I set up my lessons and learn to adapt for the needs of my diverse learners?

4. What high-stakes formal assessments are part of district expectations?

5. What formal assessments should I be creating or using this year?

6. Can you review informal assessment with me and share when you think I should be doing these assessments?

Other questions I have . . .

Anticipate Your Mentor's Questions

1. What do you already know about tests and assessment?

2. What do you already know about teaching diverse learners?

3. Share one strategy you have used that assisted a student who was struggling to learn new information.

4. What can I do to assist you right now that would reduce your anxiety?

NOVEMBER

Meetings and Observations

Plan brief weekly meetings with your mentor. The ACTs in this chapter serve as mentoring conversation starters and can also be used to assess or review what you may already know about a given topic.

Plan to meet at times that allow you to have quality time together in a place without interruptions. Knowing when you will meet each week reduces anxiety for you. You will find that you look forward to regularly scheduled meetings especially if they are short. Use this calendar to document your meetings and invite your mentor to schedule classroom visits to see you in action. There are many videos in this book and also in your mentor's *Mentoring in Action* book. Consider scheduling time to watch the videos together and have a discussion. A digital version of this calendar (November Calendar.pdf) is available on the companion website.

Review the observation requirement for novice teachers. Is your mentor planning to observe you this month? Even if he just observes for 10–15 minutes and has a short a postconference, you can learn so much. For example, just schedule a time to have your mentor observe the *opening* of a lesson to see how you give directions and get students started on a lesson. Or perhaps you would prefer your mentor observe the *closing* of a lesson if you are finding that to be more of a challenge. Find a way to get your mentor to watch you teach.

November Calendar

MONDAY	TUESDAY	WEDNESDAY	THURSDAY	FRIDAY

Use this calendar to PLAN the month with your mentor as well as to document meetings or observations.

Companion Website

CONNECT to Additional Resources

CONNECT to School and District Resources

What resources exist in your school and community that could assist you in November?

CONNECT With Colleagues, Parents, and Families

How can parents be helpful in having you understand students' learning styles?

CONNECT to Student Voices

Watch the *Qualities of Effective Teachers Through Students' Eyes* video, available on the companion website, with your mentor. Respond to these prompts together. What three things stood out for you in this video? How are these students influencing your thinking abut teaching? What will you change in your teaching as a result of watching this video?

CONNECT to Education Hot Topics

Grief Counseling! You may lose a family member or spouse while you are teaching this year. Be prepared to ask for support and help in finding resources to process your grief. You may also have students who need this support because they have loss in their family. Find out what is available for your students if this happens in your classroom this year.

CONNECT With the Companion Website

Video links, forms for this chapter, a featured book and other resources by the author are located at resources.corwin.com/mentoringinaction.

The First ACT!

Differentiating Mentoring Conversations

Teaching is complex work, and you can easily become overwhelmed. It is appropriate to customize your mentoring conversations so that your mentor is responding to your needs and skills.

Directions: Discuss the prompts with your mentor or think about them on your own. Refer to your state or district teaching standards to note a common language for teaching and summarize your key ideas in each box. Skim the ACTs for this month and decide which topics are most relevant to your needs this month.

Name_____ Date _____

Monthly Needs Assessment

1. What is going well in your classroom?	3. What would you like to improve or enhance in your practice this month?
2. How do you know your practice is working? What is your evidence of success?	4. Review the ACT overview of possible conversations for this month with your mentor. What would you like to focus on this month?

A digital version of this template (Monthly Needs Assessment Sample With Standards.pdf) is available on the companion website. Keep a copy of this assessment in your professional file.

Companion Website

NOVEMBER

Overview of the ACTs for November Conversations

Directions: Skim the ACTivities listed here and complete the pages that will forward your learning. If you are a 2+ year teacher, revisit any ACTs you already completed or try some new ACTs to stretch your thinking. Digital copies of some of the ACTs are available on the companion website.

Key Question Topic	ACTivities	PAGE
Planning	**ACT 1** **How Are Students Assessed in the Classroom and District?**	97
Planning	**ACT 2** **Linking Lesson Plans to Classroom Assessment**	98
Planning	**ACT 3** **Product or Process**	99
Tools	**ACT 4** **Formative and Summative Assessments**	100
Tools	**ACT 5** **Evidence and Documentation of Progress**	101
Students	**ACT 6** **Communicating With Students**	102
Students	**ACT 7** **Students Can Share Their Learning**	103
Students	**ACT 8** **Classroom and Behavior Management Issues**	104
Students	**ACT 9** **Looking at Student Work Together**	105
Communication	**ACT 10** **Communicating With Parents**	106

How Are Students Assessed in the Classroom and District?

Key Question: How will you learn about assessment policies?

Directions: Ask your mentor to share samples of all the district tests the students will be required to take this year. Find out what the reasons are for the tests and the impact of any testing on the teachers in the district. Also ask him to share classroom tests and quizzes he has created or used in the past and how these teacher tests inform the district tests.

1. **State Testing Initiatives**

   Does the state have a statewide testing program? What is its purpose? Are there other state tests required? Which grade levels? Ask to review a copy of the tests if they are at your grade level.

   On what standards or frameworks are the tests based?

2. **District Testing Program**

   Are the students required to pass a high school exit exam? When is it given? What is the test?

   How will this state test affect the curriculum you teach in your classroom?

   What is the purpose of these tests?

   Are these tests similar to the state tests? How?

3. **Classroom Assessment and Procedures**

   Ask your mentor to share informal assessment options with you.

   Ask your mentor to share all types of formal assessments your district is using this year with you.

NOVEMBER

Linking Lesson Plans to Assessment

Key Question: How does including assessment in a lesson plan improve teaching?

Lesson planning and assessment are linked. Remember that every lesson plan should include an assessment tool of the lesson. Tapping into prior knowledge may be part of the lesson assessment to ensure the students are learning new information. This can avoid teaching students who may already *know* the information. It also assists you in designing lessons to meet the current needs of your students. Finding out what students already know can also serve as a check-in toward the middle and near the end of the unit to let a teacher know how closely the lesson objectives are being met.

Directions: Review a lesson plan you recently created and share it with your mentor. Note where you include assessment (formal or informal) and how you tap into students' prior knowledge. Review these questions with your mentor as you share your ideas.

1. Share informal and formal assessments you have integrated into your lesson planning. List your ideas here.

2. Share strategies for assessing students' prior knowledge. List your ideas and review these others.

Here are some ideas to consider.

- Ask students to individually respond to these questions in writing.
    - *What do you already know about this topic/skill?*
    - *What do you think you know or have you heard about this topic/skill?*
    - *What would you like to learn or know?*
- Give a pretest on the topic or content
- Have students write a paragraph about what they know about the topic.

Product or Process?

Key Question: How do you select assessments for diverse learners?

Directions: How does a teacher see evidence of student achievement? Will a product illustrate the student has met the objects or will a performance be better suited to demonstrating achievement? Ask your mentor to explain the difference between *product* and *process* assessment. Remember that the assessment aligns to the lesson's objective. Review these examples with your mentor and select the ones that are most useful to you and integrate them into your lesson plans.

Product (paper/pencil)	Product (visual)	Performance Process (with or without product)
Essays	Posters	Oral reports
Book reports	Banners	Speeches
Biographies	Models	Raps
Journals	Diagrams	Dramatizations
Letters	Displays	Debates
Editorials	Videotapes or audiotapes	Songs
Scripts	Portfolios	Poems
Tests	Exhibits	Demonstrations
Research reports	Paintings	Interviews
Short answers	Photos	Skits
Position papers	Websites	News reports

Companion Website

Formative and Summative Assessments

Key Question: How are formative and summative assessments used in effective teaching?

Directions: Review the differences between formative and summative assessments with your mentor so that you understand that assessment is ongoing and should not be just done at the end of a unit.

1. Formative assessment is practice: The Rehearsals

    It is authentic, ongoing, sit beside, self-assessing, learn as we go, practice, group work, conversations, checklists, surveys, drills, practice tests. It lets the teacher know how the students are learning before the final tests.

    When should you be using formative assessments?

2. Summative assessment is final: The Opening Night of the Play

    It is the final test, the grade given to an individual student, final evaluation, judgment given at the end of the unit or term, report card grade, SAT final product, paper test, project artwork, final performance, Spanish oral exam.

    When should you be using summative assessments?

3. What should students learn?

    Discuss the following questions with your mentor.

    -   What should students have a *real understanding* of that will last and carry over?

    -   What should they be *familiar with* that can be built upon in later years?

    -   What should they have an *awareness level* of that will be built upon in later years?

    -   What should English language learners be expected to know?

    -   How do special education students' plans relate to assessment?

4. What types of rubrics need to be created and used in formative or summative assessments? Ask your mentor to share samples and discuss options with you.

Companion
Website

Evidence and Documentation of Progress

Key Question: How does an effective teacher document evidence of learning?

Directions: Ask your mentor to share the common practices of record keeping and documenting student work. Review the ideas on this page with your mentor and add ideas of your own. Be sure to ask your mentor to explain how evidence relates to assessment and lesson planning.

1. Ask your mentor to share his grade book and any digital system the district is using.

2. Review student folders or portfolio systems the school is using this year.

3. Discuss progress charts that can be placed in the room for students to see and those that you keep in your grade book.

4. Discuss multiple ways to record grades in a grade book and review it for . . .

   missing assignments

   failing quizzes or tests

   homework

5. Discuss ways color-coding with highlighters in a hard copy grade book or an online e-grade book can assist a teacher in "seeing" the big picture.

   For example, highlight in pink all the assignment grid boxes of students who have B or better grades.

   Highlight missing assignments in yellow to let the teacher scan easily and remind students.

   Highlight failing tests or quizzes in orange to alert the teacher to struggling students.

Communicating With Students

Key Question: How can you keep students informed of their progress?

Teachers use a variety of systems to communicate with their students and keep them on track. The most common processes used in schools are the progress slip and the report card. Ask your mentor to share progress slip information and report card processes with you. Progress also includes growth in behavior as well as in academics. Are there any measurements on the report card for conduct and effort?

Directions: Review the ideas on this ACT and discuss which one(s) may work in your classroom. If one system doesn't work, another can be tried at any time.

Keeping Students Informed

1. *Student mailboxes/teacher mailbox.* Teachers and students can leave notes for one another about assignments, papers due, and makeup work.

2. *Student conference.* Teacher establishes a schedule and meets with individual students privately about progress. All students meet with teacher, not just failing students.

3. *Progress chart.* A subject-related progress chart is given to each student that visually documents the number of assignments completed, scores, and projects.

4. *Warnings.* When in danger of failing, a student receives a "red" note.

5. *Compliments.* Written or verbal acknowledgment of quality work is given to students.

6. *Checklist.* Placed inside daily or weekly folders—students can see what has been checked by you and approved for credit.

7. *Progress list.* Secondary students may be instructed to maintain their own grades.

8. *Midterm progress reports.* These list completed assignments and suggestions for improvement.

9. *Student-led parent conference.* Students attend and share their progress with the parents.

Students Can Share Their Learning

Key Question: How can you implement ways for students to give feedback?

Directions: Think about ways effective teachers encourage their students to check for understanding. Discuss the following ideas with your mentor and add your own to this list.

1. Hard or Easy?

   - Ask students whether they are finding the work hard or easy. They can put thumbs up or down.

   - Hold up a green card or a red card.

   - Count the responses to get a quick sense of the response. Modify the lesson as needed.

2. What Are You Learning?

   - Take a minute at the end of each class as part of the closing to ask students to write two things they learned in class today.

   - Collect and review the responses to see what students are learning. This exercise can serve two purposes: (1) to see what they recall and (2) to let you know how to plan the next lesson.

   - Write your own prediction of how the lesson went and what they will say before reading the students' responses.

3. More Time?

   - Have students raise hands to tell the teacher whether they need more time.

   - Let students reply anonymously on paper or by putting their heads down and raising their hands.

4. Work Habits Self-Assessment

   Create a worksheet that asks students to rate their behavior or understanding.

   For example:

   - I worked hard in groups today. 1–5 (ranges from *didn't work* to *worked very hard*)

   - I understand the concepts presented. 1–5 (ranges from *don't understand* to *really understand*)

5. Teacher Assessment

   Create a survey with your mentor to assess your teaching skills. Rate each 1 to 5.

   For example:
   - My teacher presents information in a way I can understand.

   - My teacher listens to my questions.

   - There is time in class for me to practice the skill.

Classroom and Behavior Management Issues

Key Question: How can you learn how to minimize misbehavior?

Directions: List the three most common classroom misbehaviors you are facing right now and be prepared to share how you are handling them. Categorize the behaviors and see how they relate to routines, student issues, or lack of planning. Discuss how to minimize these disruptions. A digital version of this form is available on the companion website.

Misbehavior	How it is currently being handled	How to avoid it or minimize it
1.		
2.		
3.		

Companion Website

Looking at Student Work Together

Key Question: How can you learn to modify assignments and still have students achieve?

Directions: Review these four ways to differentiate for diverse learners and then review a sample of student work to see if modification would have helped the students achieve.

1. *Find out what students know.*

   This is also an opportunity to find out who exceeds standards in the classroom on this topic, so more advanced work can be given to enrich students' learning.

2. *Use varied reading levels and audio devices to teach content.*

   Vary expectations for beginning learners by limiting vocabulary or adding enrichment words.

3. *Vary the instructional method to meet diverse learning needs.*

   Using partners and small groups, or a choice of process or product assignments, graphic organizers, and varied strategies keep students engaged as well as responsive to various learning needs.

4. *Offer a variety of ways to show they have learned the content.*

   Quizzes and tests are only one way to demonstrate learning. Success in school may make the difference in students staying in school.

Bring several samples of only *one* student's work to a meeting with your mentor. Look at the work and share what you see. What "story" can be told from looking at this student's work? A form for this process is available on the companion website. Share your insights with your mentor.

What does this work say about this student?	What is the evidence for that statement?	What is the next learning step for this student? How could the work be modified for this student based on the ideas on this page?

Communicating With Parents

Key Question: How can you informally, effectively communicate with parents?

You have probably already discussed formal communication with your mentor, but it is also important to review other ways you can keep parents informed on a consistent basis. Report cards and progress slips are milestones for students, but regular communication will support the progress on these high-stakes reports.

Directions: Discuss the following ideas with your mentor and select the most useful ones for your teaching.

Informal Teacher Communication

1. *In Between Formal Progress Reports*

Sometimes there is a need to contact parents at points between the formal cycle. Students who were failing last term may be doing well now, and novice teachers need to let the parents know that their support made a difference. Or parents may want to check in to see if the student is doing better because they may need to continue the monitoring at home. Share the formats you have used to communicate progress. Do you use a note? A checklist? Ask your mentor how she would like to implement this type of system.

2. *Students Who Fail a Test or Major Project*

If a student fails a test or a major project, it is usually a good idea to tell the parents. Some teachers send the test home and require a signature, so the parents can see what was missed. If a meeting is required, then the parents know exactly what the meeting is about, and the student could also be present.

3. *The Notebook*

Many teachers use a notebook with students who have challenges with schoolwork or behavior. It goes from home to school every day or once a week. This communication from parents to teacher keeps an open line of communication.

4. *Compliment Cards, E-mails, or Phone Calls*

Don't forget that all communication is about failure or problems. Creating a system where each student's parent receives a positive message once a term is an important way to stay connected to parents.

November Novice Teacher Reflections

Directions: Complete any of these prompts to summarize your experience this month, or add your own. Compare and share your reflections with your mentor or other novice teachers in your support group. You can also reflect on these prompts in your Novice Teacher journal.

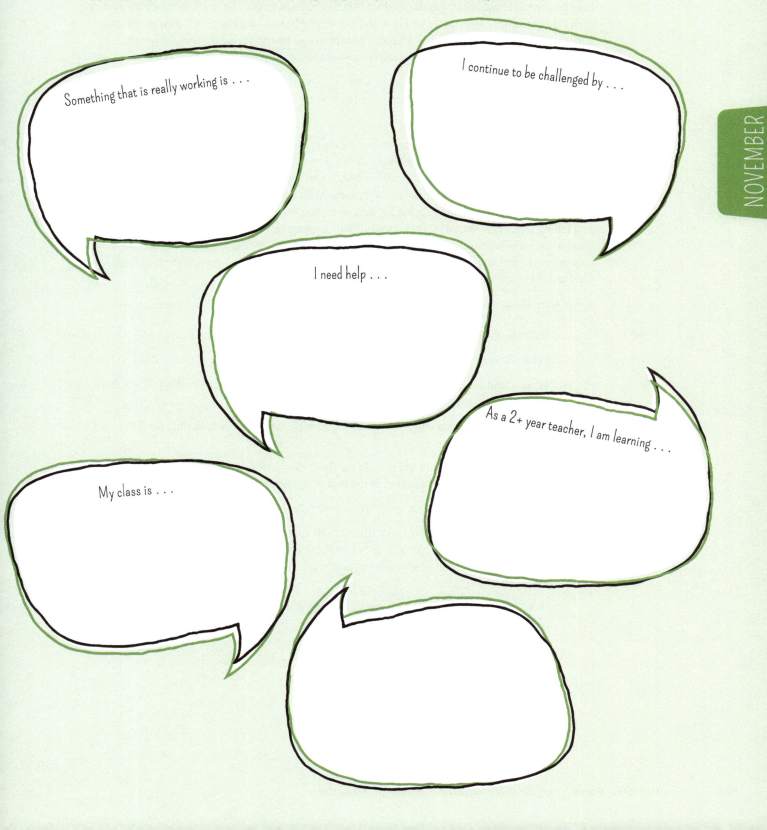

Something that is really working is . . .

I continue to be challenged by . . .

I need help . . .

As a 2+ year teacher, I am learning . . .

My class is . . .

Using Mindfulness to Explore Teaching Dilemmas

Teaching is complex, and often there are not clear answers to situations that arise while you are being mentored. The teaching dilemmas introduced at the end of each month in the REFLECT section may not always apply to you; however, the process of reflecting on this dilemma will help you think about what you might do if this did happen to you. Sometimes when a situation arises that we didn't anticipate, we react and say things before we think. This journal process will allow you to pause and think about what you would like to say next. These dilemmas are useful for mentoring conversation starters, novice teacher support group discussions, and personal reflection.

Dilemma 4: Cheating

You have been successfully assessing students' progress using both formal and informal assessments. You have reviewed the pages in the November chapter, and your mentor is pleased with your progress. You understand rubric design and are integrating informal assessment tools into your daily lesson plan. You are nervous about your test scores because they may influence your evaluation and rehiring process for next year. You are coaching your students to do well and telling them how important it is to you that they pass the tests. The students like you and want to do well. Your mentor asks you to bring your test papers to a *looking at student work* conversation, and she points out that four students have exactly the same answers on their final tests! *What do you do?*

Respond to these prompts in your Novice Teacher Journal, available on the companion website.

1. State the dilemma as clearly as possible in one sentence if you can.

2. What decision do you need to make in regard to this situation?

3. Write about the emotions that come up for you that relate to this situation. If you have two choices, write how the emotions might be different.

4. Stop and reread what you have written. Underline any key words or phrases that stand out for you.

5. Soften your eyes or close them and take three deep breaths. Ask yourself, what am I missing that I have not noticed. Write that down in your journal.

6. How can your mentor help you? Write your reflection in your journal.

7. If you are truly stuck, bring your dilemma to another novice teacher in their second or third year of teaching. Ask him or her to listen and to ask you questions to clarify your dilemma. Ask her not to give advice, just to ask you questions to help you clarify your feelings and next steps.

8. How do you feel about this dilemma now? All dilemmas are not resolved! This is a process of clarifying and understanding how you feel and how you might proceed in the future.

Directions: Complete the goal-setting processes alone or with your mentor. Write your responses on this page or in your Novice Teacher Journal, available on the companion website.

1. *Goal for Improving Your Teaching Practices*

   - Review the PLAN–CONNECT–ACT–REFLECT pages you completed in this chapter with your mentor. Look ahead to December ACTs to see what you may focus on to continue your development.

   - Acknowledge what you are learning. Write a compliment note to yourself.

   - Reflect on your teaching this month. What stands out as effective teaching? What will you do differently next month?

   - Agree on ONE goal to focus on with your mentor and reinforce your learning for next month.

   - Goal:

2. *Goal to Support Your Social and Emotional Well-Being*

   - Discuss any challenges you may be facing right now. Challenges often bring stress.

   - Don't ignore any signs of stress! Pay attention and learn ways to manage stress.

   - Continue to learn about mindfulness by reading "Educators' Social and Emotional Skills Vital to Learning," available on the companion website.

   - Goal:

"

A good teacher is someone who listens to you as a student and always tries to challenge you

—FIFTH-GRADE STUDENT

NOVICE TEACHER PHASE: CAN I DO THIS?

"I'm having trouble keeping the students on task, and I am losing valuable teaching time."

NOVICE TEACHER AFFIRMATION

I will try a variety of instructional strategies.

DECEMBER

MAINTAINING BALANCE
Teaching and Keeping the Students Interested

GUIDING QUESTIONS

1. How do you keep all learners engaged? The **Brain ACTivities** will provide ways to approach this task.

2. What do you need to know about support? The **Support ACTivities** offer you ideas to review and discuss.

3. How will you keep students central to your teaching and mentoring conversations? Use the **Student ACTivities** as a way to focus on students.

4. What is a parent communication option for this month? Use the **Communication ACTivity** as a way to connect when all is well with the student!

Interstate Teacher Assessment and Support Consortium—InTASC Standards

Review InTASC Standard 8.

- **Standard 8 Instructional Strategies**

The teacher understands and uses a variety of instructional strategies to encourage learners to develop deep understanding of content areas and their connections, and to build skills to apply knowledge in meaningful ways.

Chapter Overview

Students know good teachers. Like the fifth-grader's quote on the previous page says, "A good teacher is someone who listens to you as a student and always tries to challenge you." In this high technology world, it is a challenge to keep students' attention. Beginning teachers often don't know what students are capable of doing and may give them work that is too easy. Students want to be challenged and want to succeed. Ask your mentor to help you implement a variety of strategies that will forward student learning. Remember to listen to the students to find out what they like and how they learn best. Curriculum can be so overwhelming that you may just want to *get it done* and move on, forgetting that students need to be at the center of any curriculum work. When you feel you are losing valuable teaching time, you might get stressed out because you may not be on track to meet district goals.

If you are asking yourself, "Can I do this?" you need to meet with your mentor and find some new ways to engage your students. Maintaining your balance in December is important because it is a stressful month, and this can be a tipping point for burnout. Find ways to take short breaks and focus on your health and wellness. Social and emotional learning for adults is just as important as for students. If the adults in a school are not healthy, then it is difficult to teach students who also have their own emotional issues.

Your affirmation this month is, "I will try a variety of instructional strategies." Trying new ways to engage your learners will help you to stay focused on teaching instead of the emotional drama students present when they are not on task.

Follow the PLAN, CONNECT, ACT, REFLECT, and SET GOALS sections in this chapter to guide your mentoring conversations and reflections. Watch and listen to a mentor share her insights in Video 2.12, *Mentoring in Action: December Chapter Introduction*, on the companion website or scan the QR code on a mobile device.

VIDEO 2.12

Mentoring in Action: December Chapter Introduction

Novice Teacher Journal

One way to plan your month is to assess where you are right now. Writing in your Novice Teacher Journal will help you document what you are feeling and how to focus your teaching. A digital version of the journal is available on the companion website.

Directions: Review the chapter cover page and the overview for this month. How do this month's topic, the quotes, phase, and affirmation relate to you right now? How are you feeling as you prepare for the school year to begin? What do you feel confident about? Where do you need some help?

Use your journal to record your thoughts, feelings, and questions in a free-flowing narrative. This page is for your personal reflection; it does not need to be shared with your mentor unless you choose to do so. At the end of the year, you can review your monthly reflections to see how much you have grown.

December Entry Date_____

Today I feel . . .

_____

_____

_____

I am confident in the areas of . . .

_____

_____

_____

I need some help . . .

_____

_____

_____

Questions for Participating in Mentoring Conversations

Sometimes you don't know what to ask your mentor because you don't know what you don't know! Review this list and choose some questions that are useful to you. How will your mentor respond? Will you schedule a face-to-face meeting, or a phone appointment, or send an e-mail? What works best for both of you? Reflect on your mentor's responses and think about what works for you. If you are a 2+ year teacher, these may not all apply to you; however, there may be a question you would like to revisit.

Your Possible Questions

1. What does the district expect of me as a first year teacher?

2. Can you help me select a variety of strategies that will work for me?

3. I need help incorporating problem solving into my lessons. What should I do?

4. Critical thinking is important, but I have to cover so much content. How can I incorporate that skill into my lessons?

5. What are the successful strategies you have used that encourage students to think?

6. I am losing track of the other InTASC Principles we covered from September to November. There is so much to know. Can you review them with me?

Other questions I have . . .

Anticipate Your Mentor's Questions

1. What is working for you right now in your classroom?

2. When are your students most interested in learning?

3. What do you most enjoy about teaching, and why do you think that is so?

4. What can I do to assist you right now that would reduce your anxiety?

Meetings and Observations

Plan brief weekly meetings with your mentor. The ACTs in this chapter serve as mentoring conversation starters and can also be used to assess or review what you may already know about a given topic.

Plan to meet at times that allow you to have quality time together in a place without interruptions. Knowing when you will meet each week reduces anxiety for you. You will find that you look forward to regularly scheduled meetings especially if they are short. Use this calendar to document your meetings and invite your mentor to schedule classroom visits to see you in action. There are many videos in this book and also in your mentor's *Mentoring in Action* book. Consider scheduling time to watch the videos together and have a discussion. A digital version of this calendar (December Calendar.pdf) is available on the companion website.

You can learn a lot by observing your own teaching! One way to begin that process is using an audio recording. Record your voice using the audio setting on your phone or tablet. Before you press record, write two or three things you would like to listen for in your voice; for example, the tone of your voice, or how you use students' names, or perhaps how you give directions. You may choose to self-reflect on this recording or share it with your mentor. What did you notice?

December Calendar

MONDAY	TUESDAY	WEDNESDAY	THURSDAY	FRIDAY

Use this calendar to PLAN the month with your mentor as well as to document meetings and observations.

CONNECT to Additional Resources

CONNECT to School and District Resources

What resources exist in your school and community that could assist you in December?

CONNECT With Colleagues, Parents, and Families

How can other colleagues in the school support you in learning effective strategies for engaging students?

CONNECT to Student Voices

Watch the *Reactions to the Student Survey* video available on the companion website with your mentor. Respond to these prompts together. Would you consider conducting a student survey in your classroom? Why or why not? Would you consider sharing your survey results with your mentor? Why could this be useful? For more information about student surveys, refer to the Interactive PDF "Integrating Student Perspectives Into Mentoring Conversations" on the companion website.

CONNECT to Education Hot Topics

Homework! Read the latest research on this education matter. What is your school policy on homework? Understand the needs of homeless students in regard to assigning homework and projects. These students are struggling and need emotional support and options for fulfilling these requirements. How can you support homeless students in being successful in school?

CONNECT With the Companion Website

Video links, forms for this chapter, a featured book, and other resources by the author are located at resources.corwin.com/mentoringinaction.

The First ACT!

Differentiating Mentoring Conversations

Teaching is complex work and you can easily become overwhelmed. It is appropriate to customize your mentoring conversations so that your mentor is responding to your needs and skills.

Directions: Discuss the prompts with your mentor or think about them on your own. Refer to your state or district teaching standards to note a common language for teaching and summarize your key ideas in each box. Skim the ACTs for this month and decide which topics are most relevant to your needs this month.

Name_____ Date _____

Monthly Needs Assessment

1. What is going well in your classroom right now?	3. What would you like to improve or enhance in your practice this month?
2. How do you know your practice is working? What is your evidence of success?	4. Review the ACT overview of conversations for this month with your mentor. What would you like to focus on this month?

A digital version of this template (Monthly Needs Assessment Sample With Standards.pdf) is available on the companion website. Keep a copy of this assessment in your professional file.

Companion Website

DECEMBER

Overview of the ACTs for December Conversations

Directions: Skim the ACTivities listed here and complete the pages that will forward your learning. Digital copies of some of the ACTs are available on the companion website.

Key Question Topic	ACTivities	PAGE
Brain	ACT 1 **Problem Solving and Thinking**	119
Brain	ACT 2 **Focus on Teaching Style**	120
Brain	ACT 3 **Engage the Brain**	121
Support	ACT 4 **Revisiting Behavior Management Strategies**	122
Support	ACT 5 **Avoiding Common Problems to Keep Students Interested**	123
Support	ACT 6 **Keeping ALL Students Engaged**	124
	ACT 7 **When Is It Time to Seek Additional Support?**	125
Students	ACT 8 **Classroom and Behavior Management Issues**	126
Students	ACT 9 **Looking at Student Work Together**	127
Communication	ACT 10 **Communicating With Parents**	128

Problem-Solving and Thinking

Key Question: How can you use brain-based strategies to engage learners?

Directions: Ask your mentor to share successful strategies he has used to enhance students' problem-solving abilities. Review the ideas on this page and note where you are challenged or strong. What is your experience with brain-based strategies? Share with your mentor!

1. Critical thinking allows students to go beyond the basic memorization and to actually engage with the content. Refer to Bloom's Taxonomy and discuss with your mentor how to integrate these action verbs into lesson plans to promote higher order thinking. Review your lesson plans to note places where critical thinking can be integrated.

List your ideas here:

2. Performance skills are natural ways for students to share what they know and are able to do. Students enjoy performing plays, reading poetry, writing original stories, drawing, and dancing. Discuss ways in which these important skills can be integrated into daily lessons and units. Refer to November's Product or Process, ACT 3 section, for ideas.

List examples here:

3. Sports and games use physical activity to get the body and brain moving. Taking a short break helps students refresh and recharge. Eliminating recesses for students who are struggling actually does the opposite for their success. Think about ways you can integrate short brain-based physical movement into your lessons. Discuss how these short breaks can minimize misbehavior in students who just can't sit for long periods of time. Review a lesson plan and note where a physical break would be helpful to students.

List your ideas here:

Focus on Teaching Style

Key Question: How can a teacher's style influence student learning?

Directions: Every teacher has a preferred style of presenting information and organizing classroom resources. Answer these questions first and then interview your mentor to find out her preferred style. Your style may not match your mentor's preferred style. Your teaching style must vary to meet the needs of your students. Being mindful and aware of your teaching style means you can change it when needed. One style is not better than another and effective teachers know their preference but can use all learning styles. How the students respond to a teacher's style is what is important to learning. Asking students their preferred style is important to this process. Refer to ACT 4 in September for some reminders. An effective teacher must teach to *all* students' styles.

1. *Do you like to talk and explain concepts verbally?*

Then as a teacher, you may prefer to lecture for most of the class and hold student conferences. Students with an auditory preference will thrive in this type of classroom.

2. *Do you prefer to write and see concepts on paper?*

Then as a teacher, you probably use the board or computer to illustrate ideas. You will create written guides and require students to take notes in your classes. Students with a learning style where they prefer to write will thrive.

3. *Do you enjoy creating and showing visual displays of content?*

Then as a teacher, you will most likely be seen demonstrating concepts with models or computer displays. You may also use graphic organizers, video, and drawings to show students key ideas. Students who love to draw and use visuals will thrive.

4. *Do you like to see how things work and use your senses?*

Then as a teacher, you may design experiments and hands-on lessons using manipulatives. Students with this preference will excel in this type of classroom.

Engage the Brain

Key Question: What are some brain-based strategies you should be using?

Directions: Review any articles or professional development on brain-based teaching with your mentor. Much of what is in this book relates to the cognitive process of engaging learners but isn't specifically called brain based. Anytime you are focused on reasoning, memory, and problem solving, the brain is involved at a higher level. Even the room temperature and the way it is organized in a comfortable way influences the brain. Paying attention to all of the senses as you think about effective teaching strategies is important. Discuss these key ideas in a mentoring conversation and observe the ways you are engaging the brain to support learning in the classroom.

1. Applying learning through meaningful activities. How are you using this strategy to help students "connect" the neural networks from that lecture to an actual experience the students can relate to in life?

2. Purposefully activating prior knowledge from students can make teaching more effective. Ask your mentor to help you find easy strategies for getting at prior learning and helping students transfer what they already know to this new learning. How often have we heard students say, "We did this last year!"? Teachers cover the same content and aren't able to bring it to a higher or deeper level of understanding when they are not skilled at transferring knowledge.

3. Teaching to notice insights and big ideas makes learning exciting for students. Effective teachers know not only their content but also see the big ideas and the meaning that is often embedded in the content. Teachable moments are available every day in teaching, and we often miss them because we are too busy trying to finish the lesson or complete the objective.

4. Planning lessons and teaching units that intentionally activate cognitive learning processes is time well spent. Novice teachers often don't want to spend their time writing long lesson plans because they just want to get up and teach. You must plan clear lessons. It is crucial, and it is time worth spending.

5. Taking care of ourselves helps the brain function efficiently. Teachers often skip this! You know that there is too much to do and not enough time, but that doesn't mean we stop being healthy. You must pay attention to your own health and wellness. Set goals for social and emotional learning at the end of this chapter.

DECEMBER

Revisiting Behavior Management

Key Question: What do you need to revisit and review at this time of year?

Directions: Schedule a mentoring conversation with your mentor to discuss discipline philosophy. If misbehavior is a problem with some students, it is time for you to go back to the basics in the August and September chapters. The ACTs that didn't seem so important at the time may need to be implemented now or perhaps reviewed and revised. Ask your mentor to share his philosophy of managing misbehavior and how teachers handle disruptions differently. Discuss how respect for students is integrated into a teacher's response. Review the August CONNECT on the companion website, "What Does Respect Look Like in the Classroom?" and also ACT 8 section in October (Chapter 5) as a reminder about disciplining a student.

Incident 1. A student has forgotten his books and homework for the fifth time this year. He is failing the course and now will miss the information again. The novice teacher is frustrated and overwhelmed. *What does she do?*

Teacher A responds this way:

Teacher B responds this way:

Which response promotes future success in this class for the student?

Discuss positive appropriate ways to deal with recurring misbehavior.

Incident 2. A male student in the novice teacher's class has been bullying and bothering a girl in another class. She comes to the novice teacher for help because she knows the teacher has this student in class.

Teacher A responds this way:

Teacher B responds this way:

Which response promotes future success for the male student?

Discuss positive appropriate ways to deal with recurring misbehavior.

There is not always a clear-cut way to respond to any misbehavior. How you respond to these incidents matters and contributes to your overall philosophy of working with students who are misbehaving. Sometimes, building relationships with the most troubled students can be a very rewarding experience.

Avoiding Common Problems to Keep Students Interested

Key Question: How can you learn that common problems can be handled with solid classroom routines?

Directions: Review these key areas, assess your skill level in each area, and discuss your responses with your mentor. Effective teachers have efficient classroom management in place to minimize misbehavior.

1. *Classroom Management.* Have you structured your classroom in an orderly way to avoid potential problems? Traffic flow? Room setup? What could you change to avoid any further issues?

2. *Lesson Planning.* Have you designed lessons that meet the needs of all students so they don't get frustrated and angry when they can't succeed? Are the lessons challenging but doable? Do you have accommodations for grouping that avoid off task behavior? How can you redesign lessons to avoid problems you are experiencing?

3. *Rules, Rewards, and Consequences.* Are the rules clearly posted and understood? Do students "own" them, or are they imposed on them? Are you consistent when you apply the consequences? Do you treat all students fairly? What do you need to do to be sure your rules, rewards, and consequences are working to avoid problems?

In the review of behavior management, make sure you share with your mentor what is working and why.

Classroom Behavior	What You Are Doing	Why Is It Working?
Class members are passing in papers in an orderly way every day with their names on them!	Stopping class three minutes before the bell to allow time to pass in papers	Consistently ask students to check their names and pass in papers

Companion Website

Keeping ALL Students Engaged

Key Question: How can you be sure to include all students?

Directions: You need to continually think about ways in which to modify lessons for the diverse learners in your classroom. By December, these continual modifications get tiring, and sometimes, you just want to keep moving along with the curriculum, leaving some students behind. Review the individual education plans (IEPs) with your mentor to see if any of the students who are struggling have special needs. The strategies for teaching special needs students can be effective for all students. Review the modifications and make sure you understand them.

1. Examples of modifications:

   - Give a student more time to complete an assignment.
   - Assign fewer questions or examples to be completed.
   - Allow students to tape-record their answers instead of writing.
   - Work with a partner who would write the answers the student stated verbally.
   - Accept printed work instead of cursive.
   - Use the computer to complete work.

2. Discuss these questions:

   - How does a teacher know when to move on when there are some students who still did not learn?
   - How does a teacher pace a lesson so that all or most students complete the task?
   - How does a teacher still have high expectations for learners who work more slowly?

3. Know the students in the classroom:

   - Who needs modifications? Make a list and share it with you.
   - How can parents help?

When Is It Time to Seek Additional Support?

Key Question: How do you know when to get more support?

Directions: Students come to school with issues that are beyond your skill set. Some students are homeless, others are in need of medical and psychological help. As a beginning teacher, you can be an advocate for getting students the help they need, but often the system is complicated, and the procedures may be confusing to you. Always go to your mentor first to get advice. Together, you will decide what is in the student's best interest. You cannot do it all in your beginning years. This is not a failure on your part. Get the help you need, so you can help your students.

1. How do you know when you need more support with a student?
   - You have exhausted all existing solutions within the classroom.

   - The student continues to exhibit problems beyond the scope of common issues.

   - The mentor agrees the student needs additional help.

   - Parents have indicated a need for support.

2. What should you do?
   - Maintain accurate records of any disturbing behavior.

   - Write a request for help to the administrator in charge.

   - Document all requests for help and strategies tried in the classroom.

3. Next steps?
   - Follow up with your mentor to ensure the administrator responds.

   - Decide whether the issue requires the students in the classroom to be informed.

Classroom and Behavior Management Issues

Key Question: How do you learn how to manage degrees of inappropriate behavior?

Directions: Review the four categories below and identify appropriate responses. Add your own ideas to the list. Discuss with your mentor any recurring problems you may have with an individual student or the whole class. Notice how consequences vary depending upon the problem.

Problems	What You Need to Do
Chronic Work Avoidance Evidenced, for example, by being absent regularly, fooling around in class, not passing in assignments, tardiness.	• Make sure student is capable of work. • Keep accurate records of what is missing. • Talk with mentor teacher. • Let student know how assignments affect grade. • Talk with parents. • Other?
Habitual Rule Breaking Evidenced, for example, by calling out in class, not bringing pencil to class regularly, being talkative, forgetting other materials.	• Use consequences established. • Try behavior modification systems. • Talk with student privately. • Discuss issue with mentor teacher. • Talk with parents. • Other?
Hostile Verbal Outbursts Evidenced, for example, by angry loud yelling, chip-on-the-shoulder attitude, defiance when asked to complete assignments.	• Determine whether the outburst is just momentary. • Don't engage in a power struggle. • Remove the student if anger persists. • Talk with mentor teacher. • Talk with principal. • Talk with guidance counselor. • Talk with parents. • Other?
Fighting, Destruction, Weapons, Alcohol or Drug Abuse Evidenced, for example, by hallway pushing, violence with peers, threats, glazed look in class.	• Send a student for help. • Disperse crowds that may gather to watch. • Calmly talk; do not shout or scream. • Report the incident immediately. • Other?

Looking at Student Work Together

Key Question: How does using criteria help you rate student work effectively?

Directions: Ask your mentor to share indicators of success for student work. How does a teacher know students have learned? How does a teacher use data to analyze student work? Designing rubrics and making lists of indicators of success allows teachers to use concrete evidence to demonstrate progress. What indicators or criteria are used in your district? Complete these two processes together.

1. Randomly select a sample of student work from a completed set of papers and discuss why you think each student fits into each category. Use the rubric or criteria from the district.

Below Standard	Meets the Standard	Above Standard
What indicates that it is below standard?	What evidence shows this work meets the standard?	What makes you say it is above the standard?
Be specific in your discussion.	Check the indicators.	Be specific.

2. Complete the entire class and sort the papers into these categories. What did you learn? What is your next step for this assignment?

Below Standard	Meets the Standard	Above Standard
How many papers here?	How many papers here?	How many papers here?
% of class _____	% of class _____	% of class _____

Companion
Website

DECEMBER

Communicating With Parents

Key Question: Why is it important to share compliments with parents?

Directions: One sure way to keep students interested in school is to compliment them for what they are doing right! Parents and students love to hear good news. Because the school day is so hectic and the needs of failing students have to be a priority for a novice teacher, there often is not time to compliment the students who are doing well. Ask your mentor if she has any ideas for complimenting students.

1. Compliment Phone Calls

The goal is that every student in the class will receive a compliment within a month. Using a class list, schedule a few phone calls each night after school. Either leave a message on an answering machine or speak personally to the parents. Everyone in the class is called once a month. Be sure to keep track of any parent responses. The student actually does not know the call is coming. Keep that a surprise. Share your students' responses with your mentor! She may want to try this in her classroom, too, and compare responses. Here is a potential script for the phone calls:

> *This is an official Compliment Phone Call from Mr. Jones, Susan's teacher at Sunnyside School. I am calling to compliment your daughter for her outstanding work in class this week. She worked with other students who needed help, she answered questions in class, and she did very well on her project. Please let Susan know that she received this compliment. Have a great day!*

Keep in mind that this is not a student conference! It is a compliment for something very specific. Finding a compliment for each student may be challenging, particularly if the student has been difficult. Brainstorm some ideas together and find that good behavior or work! It will make such a difference and may even change that student's attitude in class.

2. Positive Notes

This compliment could also be given electronically as an e-mail or e-card. The key is to be specific about what is being complimented, so the student is clear about what positive behavior or academic performance is. The goal is to identify good specific behavior and reward it by telling the parents.

December Novice Teacher Reflections

Directions: Complete any of these prompts to summarize your experience this month, or add your own. Compare and share your reflections with your mentor or other novice teachers in your support group. You can also reflect on these prompts in your Novice Teacher Journal.

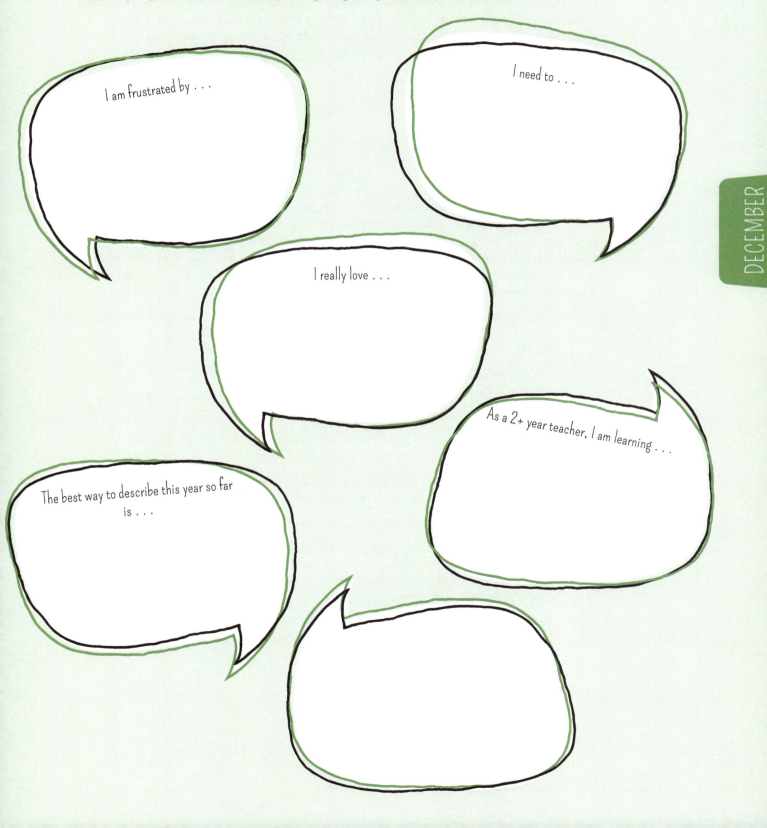

I am frustrated by . . .

I need to . . .

I really love . . .

As a 2+ year teacher, I am learning . . .

The best way to describe this year so far is . . .

Using Mindfulness to Explore Teaching Dilemmas

Teaching is complex, and often there are not clear answers to situations that arise while you are being mentored. The teaching dilemmas introduced at the end of each month in the REFLECT section may not always apply to you; however, the process of reflecting on this dilemma will help you think about what you might do if this did happen to you. Sometimes when a situation arises that we didn't anticipate, we react and say things before we think. This journal process will allow you to pause and think about what you would like to say next. These dilemmas are useful for mentoring conversation starters, novice teacher support group discussions, and personal reflection.

Dilemma 5: Took Your Advice and It Didn't Work

You came to the district with high marks from your teacher preparation program. You graduated at the top of your class in education courses. You had a successful career as an engineer, and you chose teaching because you want to give back to society and were tired of corporate business. You are enthusiastic, and you want to be a great teacher but are having trouble relating to the students. You thought they would sit and listen and care about learning. Your mentor has given you so many suggestions, and she is a terrific teacher. The students just listen to her; why don't they listen to me? You just taught a lesson using some of her ideas, and they just couldn't stop talking. You got frustrated and said, "That's it. We are not doing it! Open your books to page 20 and start answering the questions." Your mentor was in the room. You know the advice she gave was good, but you just couldn't implement it. *What do you do?*

Respond to these prompts in your Novice Teacher Journal, available on the companion website.

1. State the dilemma as clearly as possible in one sentence if you can.

2. What decision do you need to make in regard to this situation?

3. Write about the emotions that come up for you that relate to this situation. If you have two choices, write how the emotions might be different.

4. Stop and reread what you have written. Underline any key words or phrases that stand out for you.

5. Soften your eyes or close them and take three deep breaths. Ask yourself, what am I missing that I have not noticed. Write that down in your journal.

6. How can your mentor help you? Write your reflection in your journal.

7. If you are truly stuck, bring your dilemma to another novice teacher who is in her or his second or third year of teaching. Ask him or her to listen and to ask you questions to clarify your dilemma. Ask her not to give advice, just to ask you questions to help you clarify your feelings and next steps.

8. How do you feel about this dilemma now? All dilemmas are not resolved! This is a process of clarifying and understanding how you feel and how you might proceed in the future.

Directions: Complete the goal-setting processes alone or with your mentor. Write your responses on this page or in your Novice Teacher Journal, available on the companion website.

1. *Goal for Improving Your Teaching Practices*

   - Review the PLAN–CONNECT–ACT–REFLECT pages you completed in this chapter with your mentor. Look ahead to January ACTs to see what you may focus on to continue your development.

   - Acknowledge what you are learning. Create a short video on your mobile device or leave a phone message sharing what you are learning with your mentor. Thank him for his help.

   - Reflect on your teaching this month. What stood out as effective? What will you do differently next month?

   - Agree on ONE goal with your mentor to reinforce for next month.

   - Goal:

2. *Goal to Support Your Social and Emotional Well-Being*

   - Discuss any challenges you may be facing right now. Challenges often bring stress.

   - Don't ignore any signs of stress! Pay attention and learn ways to manage stress.

   - Watch the video interview with Kristen Lee Costa, available on the companion website, to learn about burnout and how you can help minimize your stress.

   - Goal:

"

I think patience makes a good teacher.

—SECOND-GRADE STUDENT

NOVICE TEACHER PHASE: REFRESHED AND READY

"I want to start the year over again because
I know so much more now."

NOVICE TEACHER AFFIRMATION

I balance my personal and professional lives.

JANUARY

BEGINNING A NEW CALENDAR YEAR

*Looking Back and
Moving Forward*

GUIDING QUESTIONS

1. How do you systematically reflect on your teaching practice? The ***Reflect ACTivities*** offer you options to think about or discuss with your mentor.

2. How do you continue to implement student voices? The ***Student ACTivities*** offer you ideas to share, try in the classroom, and discuss with your mentor

3. How can a formal agenda and meeting with parents help communication? Use the ***Communicate ACTivity*** as a way to plan a meeting.

Interstate Teacher Assessment and Support Consortium—InTASC Standards

Review InTASC Standard 9.

- **Standard 9 Professional Learning and Ethical Practice**

The teacher engages in ongoing professional learning and uses evidence to continually evaluate his/her practice, particularly the effects of his/her choices and actions on others (learners, families, other professionals, and the community), and adapts practice to meet the needs of each learner.

Chapter Overview

Patience does make a good teacher, just like the second-grade student says in the quote for January at the beginning of this chapter. Be patient with yourself. You can't learn everything in one year. If your mentor makes it look easy, don't compare yourself. You are growing and developing with each new experience and interaction with your students. Sometimes you are moving so quickly you don't even see what you are learning.

The holiday vacation may have refreshed you and this year is beginning as a "do over." Or perhaps you are second guessing your decision to teach, and you are more cautious and concerned that you can't do this work. Use this month to get back on track and set reasonable goals for yourself. New Year's resolutions are fun to make and easy to break, so be sure to create doable measurable goals. Review this month's ACT 7, "Where Is Your Sense of Humor?" Ask your mentor to guide you through this time.

Your affirmation this month is, "I balance my personal and professional lives." Some novice teachers who are committed to being excellent teachers often go overboard and focus only on work, work, work! They spend their entire vacation correcting papers, stay at school late every night, and work on weekends. This is not healthy, and it actually doesn't help. We all know there is always more work, and it is impossible to catch up. A healthy balance is required in this profession. It is okay to take a break! Review the SET GOALS section for supporting your social and emotional well-being at the end of each month. Watch Video 1.1, *Managing Your Stress to Promote Well-Being*, and Video 1.2, *Managing Your Stress: Take a Break* (see page 11), on the companion website. available on the companion website. Be a healthy role model for your students.

A professional portfolio may be required in your district or state. If it is, January is a good time to get started on reviewing the requirements. Refer back to Part I of this book to guide your thinking.

Follow the PLAN, CONNECT, ACT, REFLECT, and SET GOALS sections in this chapter to guide your mentoring conversations and reflections. Watch and listen to a mentor share her insights in the *Mentoring in Action: January Chapter Introduction* on the companion website or scan the QR code on a mobile device.

VIDEO 2.13

Mentoring
in Action:
January Chapter
Introduction

Companion
Website

Novice Teacher Journal

One way to plan your month is to assess where you are right now. Writing in your Novice Teacher Journal will help you document what you are feeling and focus your teaching. A digital version of the journal is available on the companion website.

Directions: Review the chapter cover page and the overview for this month. How do this month's topic, the quotes, phase, and affirmation relate to you right now? How are you feeling as you prepare for the school year to begin? What do you feel confident about? Where do you need some help?

Use your journal to record your thoughts, feelings, and questions in a free-flowing narrative. This page is for your personal reflection; it does not need to be shared with your mentor unless you choose to do so. At the end of the year, you can review your monthly reflections to see how much you have grown.

January Entry Date_____

Today I feel . . .

_____

_____

_____

I am confident in the areas of . . .

_____

_____

_____

I need some help . . .

_____

_____

_____

JANUARY

Questions for Participating in Mentoring Conversations

Sometimes you don't know what to ask your mentor because you don't know what you don't know! Review this list and choose some questions that are useful to you. How will your mentor respond? Will you schedule a face-to-face meeting, or a phone appointment, or send an e-mail? What works best for both of you? Reflect on your mentor's responses and think about what works for you. If you are a 2+ year teacher, these may not all apply to you; however, there may be a question you would like to revisit.

Your Possible Questions

1. I would like to share ideas and learn from others. How do I connect with other novice teachers?

2. What opportunities are available in the district, through the teachers' union, or from local professional development providers?

3. In your professional opinion, what should I focus on to improve my practice for the rest of the year?

4. Is there a way I could easily connect with the parents and the community that would assist me in my teaching?

5. Do you have any suggestions for assisting me in reflecting more systematically, so I don't lose my good ideas?

Other questions I have . . .

Anticipate Your Mentor's Questions

1. Do you keep a journal? Why or why not? How do you reflect on your practice?

2. What changes have you already made in what you are doing and why?

3. What can I do to assist you right now that would forward your teaching practice?

Meetings and Observations

Plan brief weekly meetings with your mentor. The ACTs in this chapter serve as mentoring conversation starters and can also be used to assess or review what you may already know about a given topic.

Plan to meet at times that allow you to have quality time together in a place without interruptions. Knowing when you will meet each week reduces anxiety for you. You will find that you look forward to regularly scheduled meetings especially if they are short. Use this calendar to document your meetings and invite your mentor to schedule classroom visits to see you in action. There are many videos in this book and also in your mentor's *Mentoring in Action* book. Consider scheduling time to watch the videos together and have a discussion. A digital version of this calendar (January Calendar.pdf) is available on the companion website.

Create a video of part of a lesson to share with your mentor. Using technology from the school or a portable device, make a short 10–15 minute clip of yourself in action that can provide data for a reflective conversation. If you don't want to share the clip with your mentor, just watch it and self-reflect. Be sure to get permissions from parents.

January Calendar

MONDAY	TUESDAY	WEDNESDAY	THURSDAY	FRIDAY

Use this calendar to PLAN the month with your mentor as well as to document meetings and observations.

CONNECT to Additional Resources

CONNECT to School and District Resources

What resources exist in your school and community that could assist you in January?

CONNECT With Master Teachers

Who in the professional community or district inspires professional growth and reflection? Ask your mentor to set up a meeting with one or more of these teachers. Read "25 Things Excellent Teachers Do Differently" on TeachThought.com and review the advice with your mentor to see what you might like to try in your classroom.

CONNECT to Student Voices

Student choice is another way to include student voice in the classroom. Refer to the form titled "How Can Student Choice Help Learning?" available on the companion website and share these ideas with your mentor. Create a sociogram if you have never done this before. Use ACT 5 in this chapter and also search the web for samples and directions about this useful tool. Think about how you use student choice in your classroom.

CONNECT to Education Hot Topics

Attendance matters! Students who come to school regularly have a better chance of retaining learning, succeeding in school, and socializing within society. Search for attendance motivators with your mentor and think of some ways to reward attendance. It saves you a lot of work doing makeup if students show up to class every day!

CONNECT With the Companion Website

Video links, forms for this chapter, a featured book, and other resources by the author are located at resources.corwin.com/mentoringinaction.

The First ACT!

Differentiating Mentoring Conversations

Teaching is complex work and you can easily become overwhelmed. It is appropriate to customize your mentoring conversations so that your mentor is responding to your needs and skills.

Directions: Discuss the prompts with your mentor or think about them on your own. Refer to your state or district teaching standards to note a common language for teaching and summarize your key ideas in each box. Skim the ACTs for this month and decide which topics are most relevant to your needs this month.

Name_____ Date _____

Monthly Needs Assessment

1. What is going well in your classroom right now?	3. What would you like to improve or enhance in your practice this month?
2. How do you know your practice is working? What is your evidence of success?	4. Review the ACT overview of possible conversations for this month with your mentor. What would you like to focus on this month?

A digital version of this template (Monthly Needs Assessment Sample With Standards.pdf) is available on the companion website. Keep a copy of this assessment in your professional file.

Overview of the ACTs for January Conversations

Directions: Skim the ACTivities listed here and complete the pages that will forward your learning. If you are a 2+ year teacher, revisit any ACTs you already completed or try some new ACTs to stretch your thinking. Digital copies of some of the ACTs are available on the companion website.

Key Question Topic	ACTivities	PAGE
Reflect	ACT 1 **Looking Back**	141
Reflect	ACT 2 **Moving Forward**	142
Reflect	ACT 3 **What Do I Believe?**	143
Reflect	ACT 4 **Self-Reflection**	144
Students	ACT 5 **Constructing a Sociogram**	145
Students	ACT 6 **Using Drawings to Gain Student Perspective**	146
Students	ACT 7 **Where Is Your Sense of Humor?**	147
Students	ACT 8 **Classroom and Behavior Management Issues**	148
Students	ACT 9 **Looking at Student Work Together**	149
Communicate	ACT 10 **Communicating With Parents**	150

Looking Back

Key Question: How can you systematically reflect on the first half of the year?

Directions: Think about your successes and challenges for the first part of the year. Ask your mentor to also share what she feels and just listen to what she has to say. Select one of the following activities and write a reflection in your Novice Teacher Journal.

1. Self-Reflection

Write a letter to yourself that highlights areas of growth, new insights about teaching and learning, or successes. Also include one challenge you are facing that you would like to discuss at a future meeting. Also share what you would like to be acknowledged for so far this year. Indicate one goal you have for the second half of the year. Consider handwriting the letter to slow yourself down a bit and allow the reflective process to emerge. Sign and date your letter. Look back at this letter at the end of the year.

Note: If the challenge you list relates to one student in the classroom, consider doing this reflective process as well.

2. A Student's Perspective

Write an imaginary essay from the perspective of the most difficult student in your classroom. Yes that one! In this process, pretend you are the student. Your teacher has required you to write a journal entry about your life and success in school.

Begin the journal by writing "Dear Diary, Today I am in school and. . . . My teacher thinks. . . . My life at home is . . . ." Sign the student's name at the end.

This is a very powerful process and is especially enlightening when you put yourself in one of your student's shoes. It is an imagined response, and you may not have any idea what this student would think or say. The purpose of the exercise is to guess why a student like this would behave in these ways. Just go with the flow on this one. See what emerges from this student.

You may choose to share these with your mentor or just keep them for your own personal reflection.

JANUARY

Companion
Website

Moving Forward

Key Question: How can you support yourself so that you can move forward?

Directions: Sometimes you may find yourself worrying. Your challenges can become struggles, and you have tried many ideas, and they just might not be working for you. One way to move forward is to use this process. Sometimes all it takes is to see "possibilities" in these problems. Some issues are out of your control. Finding strategies for letting go of issues you can't do anything about is important at this time of year. This process works best in a small group, but you can do it with your mentor.

Problems to Possibilities

1. Write your most challenging problems or worries on *blue* sticky notes (the color symbolizes what makes you feel challenged or "blue"). Then classify the problems into categories (e.g., student misbehavior, managing paperwork, organizing the room, parent issues) and write that on the top of the sticky note. Share the problems with your mentor or other novice teachers.

2. Place the blue problems on a Worry Wall at the front of the room in categories as defined by the classifications at the top of the sticky notes.

3. Walk up to the wall and read all the problems and think about the possible solutions to any of them. Using *yellow* sticky notes, you and the teachers in your support group can place possible solutions on any problems.

4. If you are doing this in a group, the person who originally placed the problems on the wall now goes back and picks them up with the solutions attached to them. Discuss the possibilities that emerged from the process.

Debrief: Your goal is to see the possible solutions to existing challenges and to also recognize what you can't do anything about. You may need to find additional support for some issues. Working in a group will also show you that other teachers have similar problems, and you can help each other.

What Do I Believe?

Key Question: How can you document your beliefs?

Directions: At this time of year, it is important to revisit your philosophy statement. You probably wrote one for your college application or for this teaching position. What you may have believed before actually teaching could be different from what you believe now that you are in the classroom. If you never wrote a philosophy statement, this is a good time to do one. Respond to the following prompts.

1. List three words that describe you as a teacher.

   The first words that come to mind . . .

2. List three words your students would use to describe you as a teacher.

   The first three that come to mind . . .

   How do these words compare?

   Why are they alike or different?

3. Now think about your beliefs about teaching and learning. Complete this prompt twice.

   I believe . . .

   I also believe . . .

4. Finally, list one way you are demonstrating what you believe in the classroom. What are you doing that shows what you believe in or who you are (as described in your descriptive words)?

5. How have any of your beliefs changed since the beginning of the year? Do your beliefs match your teaching strategies?

Self-Reflection

Key Question: What can you learn by completing a reflection on a lesson?

Directions: One powerful activity at this time of year is to look at your practice in a formal way. When you systematically take time to reflect on your practice, you may begin to see what is working and how to modify your instruction. Select one lesson to assess in depth. Schedule a time to review your reflections with your mentor.

Lesson Title:_____ Date _____

1. Did the students learn from my lesson? Were they actively engaged? How do I know?

2. How closely did I follow my lesson plan? Did I have to modify during the lesson? Why?

3. What do I think was the most effective part of the lesson?

4. Were the materials/visuals/aids appropriate? Why? Why not?

5. What would I change/keep the same the next time I do this lesson?

6. What do I see as my teaching strengths?

7. What are my next steps?

8. What have I learned about my teaching practice by doing this lesson's reflection?

Constructing a Sociogram

Key Question: How does knowing what students think about each other inform a teacher's practice?

Directions: Explore the types of sociogram options online. A sociogram illustrates the dynamics in a classroom visually, so you can see who the stars and isolates are in your classroom. By having this information, you can be more aware of tensions or friendships in the classroom. Ask your mentor to help in doing this process. It is amazing what information is gained that you can use for grouping and learning about your students.

Sample Sociogram Process

Step 1 Ask students in the classroom to list three students, by first, second, and third choice, whom they would prefer to work with in the classroom. (Make a distinction between work partners and social partners outside of school.) Tell them it is for possible future group projects and that you may use it to try and create teams with at least one person they prefer to work with.

Step 2 Have the students write why they selected each student. This will give you some insight, and themes may repeat themselves.

Step 3 Collect the data and make a grid with students' names across the top and down the left side. Graph paper works well. Place a 1, 2, or 3 under the student's name as indicated to show choices.

Step 4 Tally choices to indicate most preferred working partners (commonly called *stars*) and least selected working partners (referred to as *isolates*).

	Sue	David	Adam	Kat
Sue	—	1	3	2
David	3	—	1	2
Adam	3	2	—	1
Kat	3	2	1	—

JANUARY

Using Drawings to Gain Student Perspective

Key Question: How can a visual representation of a teacher illustrate what students think?

Directions: One way to capture perspectives is to have the students draw a picture of the classroom or the teacher. Review these prompts and select one with your mentor that would be a good fit for you. Younger students love to draw their teachers. High school students may find this boring, but some may like the opportunity to express themselves in a different way. Here are some basic prompts. Feel free to create one of your own!

1. Draw a picture of your teacher (leave it very general—see what students do).

2. Draw a picture of your teacher in the classroom (again, leave it general—just in the classroom).

3. Draw one picture of your teacher teaching (keep it general).

4. Draw a picture of the classroom (don't mention the teacher). See if they put the teacher in or not.

5. Draw a picture of yourself (the student) in the classroom (this would give some insight as to what the student thinks).

6. Draw a picture of yourself (the student) learning something in the classroom.

Obviously, the directions for younger students may have to be more explicit. Some teachers might say, if a camera were brought into this room, what would it see? Draw a picture (i.e., a snapshot of the classroom to capture what it looks like) just like the camera would. Explain to the students that this assignment is being given to allow them to express their ideas in a different way instead of giving a written survey.

Debrief: Discuss the completed drawings and look for themes or interesting illustrations. Together you can note how you are portrayed. Is the teacher standing up front saying "sit down" or "stop talking," or is she at her desk reading, or perhaps the teacher isn't even in the room? This is just one unique way to capture perspectives. Consider comparing what you learn with your sociogram data.

Where Is Your Sense of Humor?

Key Question: How can you see the funny side of teaching?

Directions: Most of your mentoring meetings are probably spent trying to resolve issues, share challenges, and discuss problems. Even though there is a place for acknowledgment, it often gets buried by pressing emotional worries you bring to the table. So what is fun about teaching? Sometimes the kids say hysterical things or respond to questions in a funny way. As long as respect is part of the process, it is ok to laugh! Sometimes we just take it all so seriously! Where is the joy in teaching?

Remember that talking about students, their parents, or any other school issue is not appropriate at any event. We all have had an experience where we have heard gossip and inappropriate information being transferred about students. Professionalism and confidentiality must be a priority. Have fun but not at others' expense. Using humor does not mean "making fun of" someone else. Find the fun in teaching.

Review these activities and consider doing one.

1. Invite your mentor to share how she uses humor in the classroom with students. Students like teachers who laugh and make learning fun.

2. Schedule a social activity for you and your mentor and talk about other things besides school! Try it!

3. Organize a movie night or social activity just for other novice teachers and their mentors. Choose a comedy!

4. Create a social directory for novice teachers in the district, so you can network and socialize!

5. Plan some free time to exercise and move!

Classroom and Behavior Management Issues

Key Question: How can you brainstorm solutions to your common problems?

Directions: Read the case with your mentor and discuss how each situation could be handled. Expand the details of the case by adding some grade-level context so that it is meaningful to you. Brainstorm at least three possible ways a teacher could respond. Ask your mentor, what would he do if this happened in his classroom? Remember you don't have to do everything the same way as your mentor. It is just good to know what his perspective is related to these issues.

Case 1: The Class Clown

The class clown comes in late and tells jokes every day during class. Everyone loves her and laughs so hard it is difficult to get their attention. Valuable class time is being wasted.

Case 2: The Bully

This girl hits at least one person a day. She walks by people and punches their arms, or she trips anyone who walks by her desk. She is the terror of the playground.

Case 3: The Lie

A very likable student who always completed his homework lied and said he had handed it in one day. The teacher discovered he had not done it at all and just called out YES when she asked students during roll call.

Case 4: A Destructive Student

A very quiet student exhibits aggressive behavior by quietly breaking pencils at his desk while the teacher is giving the directions.

Case 5: Shouting Out

This student is so excited and wants to participate in class discussions. She always shouts out the answers when the teacher asks the class general questions. No one else has a chance to even talk.

Case 6: Sleeper

This student slumps over his desk in the back of the room. He is not disturbing anyone, but he is not learning the material either. He is in danger of failing the class.

Case 7: Cheating

A student was caught cheating on a test. The answers were clearly on her hand, and she was copying them onto her paper. She had cheated before and at that time had said she would not do it again.

Case 8: A Fist Fight

Two students hit each other in the hallway outside the teacher's door about a personal issue. No one is hurt, but a group of students is surrounding them.

Looking at Student Work Together

Key Question: How can you find common errors students are making?

Directions: Bring a set of completed and corrected papers to a meeting with your mentor. Sort the papers into these categories or into the categories in the rubric you are using in your district. Discuss the importance of taking time to analyze errors to see if a reteach of a lesson could move students to higher learning.

Below Standard	Meets the Standard	Above Standard
How many papers here?	How many papers here?	How many papers here?
% of class _____	% of class _____	% of class _____

1. Look at all the papers in the Below Standard category or the lowest category in your rubric.

   Is there a pattern illustrating common errors students are making?

   What could you do next to move these students to Meets the Standard category?

2. Look at all the papers in the Meets the Standard category.

   Is there a pattern for errors?

   What could you do next to move these students to Above Standard?

Companion Website

Communicating With Parents

Key Question: How can organized parent meetings help students learn?

Directions: This is a new year, and you are hopefully revitalized. This is a good time to schedule a meeting with your students' parents to share what is going on in your classroom. The purpose of the meeting is about how you and the parents can work together to support this student's learning. Make sure you let the parents know this is not a "failing" meeting but rather a "support" meeting so the student will not fail.

Sample Meeting Agenda

1. **Opening the Meeting (options to consider)**
   - I am so glad you could join me today in discussing John's progress.
   - The purpose of this meeting is . . .
   - Can you tell me some things that are going on at home or outside of school right now . . .
   - You know your child better than I do; can you give me some insights, so I can help him be successful in school?

2. **Sharing the Positive**
   - This is what I see going well for John right now . . .
   - This sample of work shows he can . . .
   - I also know that John is very good at . . .

3. **Standards and Curriculum Goals**
   - These are the learning goals for ____ grade this year.
   - Let's look at the areas where John needs assistance. By the end of the year, John needs to meet _____ standards
   - My concerns for John are . . .

4. **Working Together to Set Goals**
   - How can we assist John together?
   - One thing you could do at home is . . .
   - When should we meet again to check on John's progress?

5. **Closing the Meeting on a Positive Note**
   - Thanking parents for attending.
   - Praising them for their support.

January Novice Teacher Reflections

Directions: Complete any of these prompts to summarize your experience this month. Compare and share your reflections with your mentor or other novice teachers in your support group. You can also reflect on these prompts in your Novice Teacher Journal.

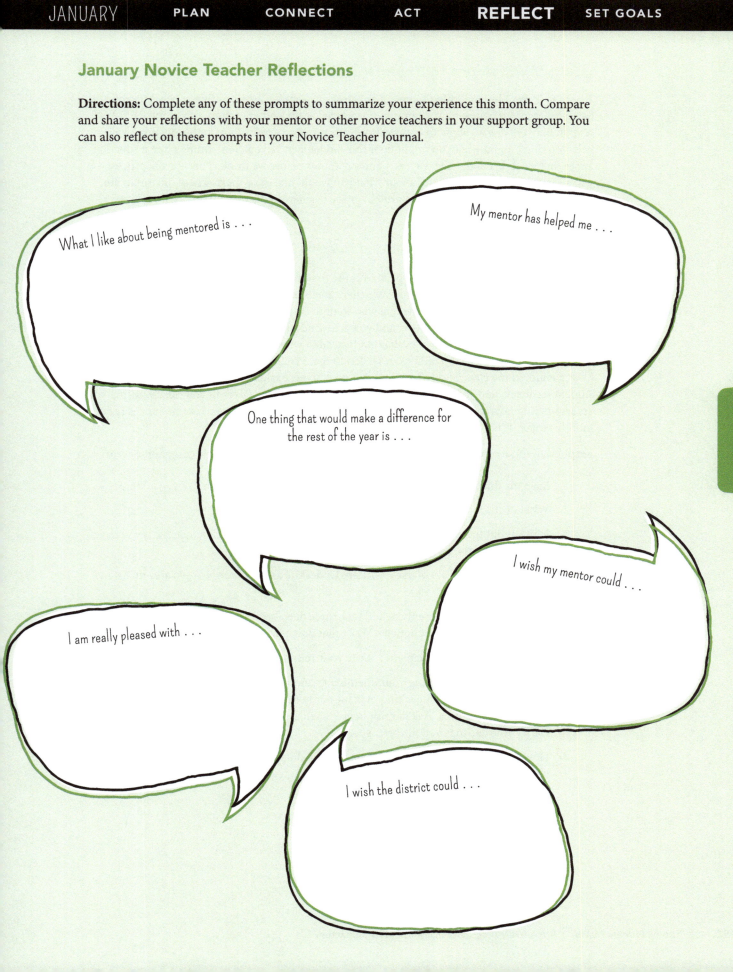

What I like about being mentored is . . .

My mentor has helped me . . .

One thing that would make a difference for the rest of the year is . . .

I am really pleased with . . .

I wish my mentor could . . .

I wish the district could . . .

JANUARY

Using Mindfulness to Explore Teaching Dilemmas

Teaching is complex, and often there are not clear answers to situations that arise while you are being mentored. The teaching dilemmas introduced at the end of each month in the REFLECT section may not always apply to you; however, the process of reflecting on this dilemma will help you think about what you might do if this did happen to you. Sometimes when a situation arises that we didn't anticipate, we react and say things before we think. This journal process will allow you to pause and think about what you would like to say next. These dilemmas are useful for mentoring conversation starters, novice teacher support group discussions, and personal reflection.

Dilemma 6: Doesn't Matter What the Students Think

It is January, and it is time to reflect back over the first months of the year and your progress. You have been wondering why so many teachers, including your mentor, care so much about what the students think. You are the one who went to college to become a teacher. It is the principal who will be evaluating you, and you are wondering why your mentor isn't spending some time preparing you for that evaluation instead of what the students' think about you. You are thinking, if they just stop talking and listen to me, I could teach; and then there wouldn't be any issues in my classroom! You know that your state's evaluation system is moving toward student feedback, and you have always included students' perspectives in your teaching, but you are wondering how this is supposed to help you become a better teacher. Your mentor is really into this topic. *What do you do?*

Respond to these prompts in your Novice Teacher Journal, available on the companion website.

1. State the dilemma as clearly as possible in one sentence if you can.

2. What decision do you need to make in regard to this situation?

3. Write about the emotions that come up for you that relate to this situation. If you have two choices, write how the emotions might be different.

4. Stop and reread what you have written. Underline any key words or phrases that stand out for you.

5. Soften your eyes or close them and take three deep breaths. Ask yourself, what am I missing that I have not noticed. Write that down in your journal.

6. How can your mentor help you? Write your reflection in your journal.

7. If you are truly stuck bring your dilemma to another novice teacher who is in his or her second or third year of teaching. Ask him or her to listen and to ask you questions to clarify your dilemma. Ask her not to give advice, just to ask you questions to help you clarify your feelings and next steps.

8. How do you feel about this dilemma now? All dilemmas are not resolved! This is a process of clarifying and understanding how you feel and how you might proceed in the future.

Directions: Complete all three goal-setting processes alone or with your mentor. Write your responses on this page or in your Novice Teacher Journal, available on the companion website.

1. *Goal for Improving Your Teaching Practices*

   - Review the PLAN–CONNECT–ACT–REFLECT pages you completed in this chapter with your mentor. Look ahead to February ACTs to see what you may focus on to continue your development.

   - Acknowledge what you are learning. Give yourself a pat on the back! What are you doing well?

   - Reflect on your teaching this month. What stood out as effective? What will you do differently next month?

   - Agree on ONE goal with your mentor to reinforce for next month.

   - Goal:

2. *Goal to Support Your Social and Emotional Well-Being*

   - Discuss any challenges you may be facing right now. Challenges often bring stress.

   - Don't ignore any signs of stress! Pay attention and learn ways to manage stress.

   - Watch Video 1.2, *Managing Your Stress: Take a Break* (see page 11), available on the companion website, to learn how to take a break at school and minimize your stress.

   - Goal:

JANUARY

"

What I think makes a good teacher is that they can teach all kinds of things your parents don't know.

—SIXTH-GRADE STUDENT

NOVICE TEACHER PHASE: STAYING FOCUSED

"There is so much to teach before the end of the school year. How will I do it all?"

NOVICE TEACHER AFFIRMATION

I bring optimism to my classroom.

FEBRUARY

ENGAGING STUDENTS IN THE CURRICULUM

Focus on Content Through Active Inquiry

GUIDING QUESTIONS

1. How do I create a community of learners? The **Reflect ACTivities** will provide ways to approach this task.

2. How will I include students' voices in the classroom? Use the **Student ACTivities** as a way to think about the options for engaging students.

3. Why is it important to tell parents what their students are learning in class? Use the **Communicate ACTivity** as a way to focus on how to update parents on classroom content.

Interstate Teacher Assessment and Support Consortium—InTASC Standards

Review InTASC Standards 4 and 5.

- **Standard 4 Content Knowledge**

The teacher understands the central concepts, tools of inquiry, and structures of the discipline(s) he or she teaches and creates learning experiences that make these aspects of the discipline accessible and meaningful for learners to ensure mastery of the content.

- **Standard 5 Application of Content**

The teacher understands how to connect concepts and use differing perspectives to engage learners in critical thinking, creativity, and collaborative problem solving related to authentic local and global issues.

Chapter Overview

There is so much to do at this time of year that you might just get very scattered and not know what to do first. Break the curriculum down into bite-sized pieces, so you can understand what the next steps could be and how you should implement them. The curriculum usually is the most challenging part of the first year because you are teaching it for the first time.

At this time of year, it is important to just stay focused on teaching. As the quote for this chapter says, "What I think makes a good teacher is that they can teach all kinds of things your parents don't know." Remember you do know things! All of this is not new to you.

This month highlights the continued use of varied teaching strategies as well as the opportunity to give students choices in the classroom. When a teacher gives options to students about what they can do for homework, for example, the students have to engage in the conversation and commit to something. It is more likely they will actually do their homework if they selected it! Ultimately, it may not matter which homework assignment is completed or how the content is learned.

The affirmation for this month is, "I bring optimism to my classroom." By focusing on what is working and what you bring to teaching, you highlight your strengths. Optimism brings hope and a sense that you *can* teach effectively.

Follow the PLAN, CONNECT, ACT, REFLECT, and SET GOALS sections in this chapter to guide your mentoring conversations and reflections. Watch and listen to a mentor share her insights in Video 2.14, *Mentoring in Action: February Chapter Introduction*, on the companion website or scan the QR code on a mobile device.

VIDEO 2.14

Mentoring in Action: February Chapter Introduction

FEBRUARY

Novice Teacher Journal

One way to plan your month is to assess where you are right now. Writing in your Novice Teacher Journal will help you document what you are feeling and how to focus your teaching. A digital version of the journal is available on the companion website.

Directions: Review the chapter cover page and the overview for this month. How do this month's topic, the quotes, phase, and affirmation relate to you right now? How are you feeling as you prepare for the school year to begin? What do you feel confident about? Where do you need some help?

Use your journal to record your thoughts, feelings, and questions in a free-flowing narrative. This page is for your personal reflection; it does not need to be shared with your mentor unless you choose to do so. At the end of the year, you can review your monthly reflections to see how much you have grown.

February Entry Date_____

Today I feel . . .

_____

_____

_____

I am confident in the areas of . . .

_____

_____

_____

I need some help . . .

_____

_____

_____

FEBRUARY

Questions for Participating in Mentoring Conversations

Sometimes you don't know what to ask your mentor because you don't know what you don't know! Review this list and choose some questions that are useful to you. If you are a 2+ year teacher, these may not all apply to you; however, there may be a question you would like to revisit.

Your Possible Questions

1. How do I get the students to support each other and work together?

2. Are there easy ways to integrate media and audiovisual aids into my lessons?

3. I want to foster active inquiry in my lessons, but it just gets too complicated. Can you suggest some teachers I could observe who use this technique to engage their students?

4. I feel like I am talking too much. What are some nonverbal ways I could communicate with my students that will create a supportive environment for learning?

Other questions I have . . .

Anticipate Your Mentor's Questions

1. What are your goals for creating a collaborative learning environment?

2. How do you communicate these goals to your students?

3. What would you do if you could do anything in your classroom right now?

4. What can I do to assist you right now that would reduce your anxiety?

FEBRUARY

Meetings and Observations

Plan brief weekly meetings with your mentor. The ACTs in this chapter serve as mentoring conversation starters and can also be used to assess or review what you may already know about a given topic.

Plan to meet at times that allow you to have quality time together in a place without interruptions. Knowing when you will meet each week reduces anxiety for you. You will find that you look forward to regularly scheduled meetings especially if they are short. Use this calendar to document your meetings and invite your mentor to schedule classroom visits to see you in action. There are many videos in this book and also in your mentor's *Mentoring in Action* book. Consider scheduling time to watch the videos together and have a discussion. A digital version of this calendar (February Calendar.pdf) is available on the companion website.

If you have not already done so, schedule a time to have your mentor observe you for an entire class period this month. Tell your mentor what you would like her to look for during the class. Focus on one or two areas, so you are not overwhelmed with data. Make sure you have a postconference, so you can get some feedback. Share what you like about the feedback so that it will be most useful to you.

February Calendar

MONDAY	TUESDAY	WEDNESDAY	THURSDAY	FRIDAY

Use this calendar to PLAN the month with your mentor as well as to document meetings and observations.

FEBRUARY

CONNECT to Additional Resources

CONNECT to School and District Resources

What resources exist in your school and community that could assist you in February?

CONNECT With Colleagues, Parents, and Families

Who in the professional community could assist you with ideas for engaging students?

How can parents be used as resources for sharing content?

CONNECT to Student Voices

How a classroom is organized and what it "feels" like to students matters. Review the ideas on the form "How Does Classroom Space Influence Learning," available on the companion website, to discuss physical space issues in your classroom. Test some of these ideas!

CONNECT to Education Hot Topics

Engage students with videos and feature films! Discuss the policies for using online clips and feature films in the classroom in your district. Using a study guide so students know what to look for in the film guides helps you to use the video appropriately. It also demonstrates to the principal that this is time on task.

CONNECT With the Companion Website

Video links, forms for this chapter, a featured book, and other resources by the author are located at resources.corwin.com/mentoringinaction.

The First ACT!

Differentiating Mentoring Conversations

Teaching is complex work, and you can easily become overwhelmed. It is appropriate to customize your mentoring conversations so that your mentor is responding to your needs and skills.

Directions: Discuss the prompts with your mentor or think about them on your own. Refer to your state or district teaching standards to note a common language for teaching and summarize your key ideas in each box. Skim the ACTs for this month and decide which topics are most relevant to your needs this month.

Name_____ Date _____

Monthly Needs Assessment

1. What is going well in your classroom right now?	3. What would you like to improve or enhance in your practice this month?
2. How do you know your practice is working? What is your evidence of success?	4. Review the ACT overview of possible conversations for this month with your mentor. What would you like to focus on this month?

A digital version of this template (Monthly Needs Assessment Sample With Standards.pdf) is available on the companion website. Keep a copy of this assessment in your professional file.

Companion Website

Overview of the ACTs for February Conversations

Directions: Skim the ACTivities listed here and complete the pages that will forward your learning. Digital copies of some of the ACTs are available on the companion website.

Key Question Topic	ACTivities	PAGE
Reflect	ACT 1 **Using Varied Teaching Strategies**	163
Reflect	ACT 2 **How Much Time?**	164
Reflect	ACT 3 **Engaging Learners**	165
Students	ACT 4 **Student Choices to Enhance Learning**	166
Students	ACT 5 **Homework: Does It Work?**	167
Students	ACT 6 **Classroom and Behavior Management Issues**	168
Students	ACT 7 **Looking at Student Work Together**	169
Communicate	ACT 8 **Communicating With Parents**	170

FEBRUARY

Using Varied Teaching Strategies

Key Question: How many different teaching strategies are you using?

Directions: Reflect with your mentor to assess how you are meeting the needs of the diverse learners in your classroom. Review our preferred teaching style in the December, or Chapter 7, ACT 2 section and discuss how you are expanding your style to include the students who may have a different learning style.

1. **Are you using both auditory and visual directions?** Students in the classroom may prefer auditory or visual directions to ensure everyone understands what to do. An effective teacher does both. By writing the directions on the board or displaying them on the computer, the teacher makes the assignment visible and available for late-arriving students.

2. **Are you demonstrating key concepts by using visual examples?** After directions are given and the novice teacher feels students understand the directions, specific examples should be given to concretely show what is expected. This does not mean students are supposed to copy the example. It is to provide a visual prop that is used by the teacher to demonstrate what is expected.

3. **Are you allowing for student choice when appropriate?** For example, if the goal is to solve a word problem in math, choices for solving could include paper and pencil, manipulatives, working alone, or working with a partner. The point is for students to use their best learning style to complete the assignment. Do you know how to do this?

4. **Are you allowing for different learning paces?** Students think and work at different speeds. The faster thinkers are not necessarily the most accurate or the most creative problem solvers. Your mentor may have encouraged (and thus fooled) you into rewarding only the quickest students because when you correct the papers, you might find they do not have the correct answers or most creative solutions. Slower paced learners or learning does not mean learners are not smart or creative. You also have to think of additional activities for those students who complete their work early. That is a common problem that you two can discuss.

5. **Are you assisting students who need support?** Some students will need additional support during a lesson because they do not understand the directions or are unable to complete the task. You may not have time to walk around the room and meet with these students individually. One strategy is to let them work with a partner who is able to explain more clearly what is expected. These "partner coaches" can be selected before class begins, and they do not have to have their own work done to assist.

FEBRUARY

Companion Website

How Much Time?

Key Question: How do you learn how to pace a lesson?

Directions: Ask your mentor to observe you and record the start and end times for each part of a lesson. Discuss what you learned and make adjustments to ensure this is enough time for student learning.

Sample			
Topic	**Time Starts**	**Time Ends**	**Total**
Introduction to lesson			
Giving directions			
Lecturing			
Answering questions			
Asking questions			
Practice work			
Reprimanding			
Checking for understanding			
Students actively engaged/ demonstrating learning			

Debrief

1. What took up the most time during the lesson?

2. What took up the least time during the lesson?

3. What stands out for you when you see the data?

Engaging Learners

Key Question: How well are you engaging all learners?

Directions: Review this list of ideas and select the two that stand out as the most important. Discuss them with your mentor or reflect on your own.

1. Create a classroom where students ask and answer questions. In most classrooms, the teacher asks a question, and the same students raise their hands and get called on. Other students are silent, and the class becomes a boring back and forth with the teacher and a few students. What if the students wrote the questions and other students answered them? How can you create this kind of environment? More engagement, fewer distracted students.

2. Create opportunities for project-based learning. Let your students create teams and show you what they know by working together on a common task. Let your mentor help you design an assessment tool that measures work quality as well as effort.

3. Have students correct their own papers. Design a process where students get to assess how sure they are their answers are correct before they pass their work in. For example, if they are 100 percent sure the answer is correct, they put a C next to their answer. If they are not sure, they put a NS or perhaps 50 percent. By looking back at their own work, they can assess how sure they are about their responses. This requires the brain to work in a different way and the students stay engaged.

4. Create an emotionally safe classroom environment. Discuss ways to do this with your mentor. You might consider setting rules and guidelines on manners for your class, such as, "We don't talk about anyone in this class, and we don't say shut up, or laugh at others." A respectful classroom allows for students to feel safe; then they can engage in learning. By including compliments from students to students during the day, the novice teacher can ensure students feel good about themselves.

Student Choices to Enhance Learning

Key Question: How can student choice motivate and engage learners?

Directions: Think about ways you can integrate choice into your lessons to motivate the unmotivated learner. Students usually know how they learn best, and if you can offer them a variety of ways in which to show you that they know the material, they will feel more successful and will be more invested in the work. Discuss with your mentor how this can be particularly useful for students whose first language is not English or students with special needs. Ask your mentor to share how she uses student choice in her classroom.

1. Examples of ways choice can be incorporated into a classroom.
   - Choosing a homework assignment from three that are acceptable.
   - Choosing a partner to work with on a project.
   - Choosing an independent reading book.
   - Choosing the type of test (multiple choice, essay, short answer).
   - Creating a test by choosing all the items that would go on the test.

2. Brainstorm with your mentor on other ways to incorporate choice to promote interest and enthusiasm in the content.

3. Discuss how options for completing a learning task could create more interest in demonstrating learning. For example, students could choose to . . .
   - Use paper and pencil
   - Use manipulatives
   - Draw the answer
   - Work alone
   - Work with a partner
   - Act out the answer
   - Use a mobile device
   - Make a video

FEBRUARY

Homework: Does It Work?

Key Question: What do you need to know about homework?

Directions: Discuss homework policies with your mentor. Review the following questions with her and share your opinion of homework and its value.

1. Do students have to pass in homework? Is it always required?

2. Does homework relate only to the content?

3. Do students get to select homework activities?

4. Is homework extra credit or required?

5. Does homework "count" and get corrected by the teachers in the school?

6. Can homework be "extra credit" for students who are really motivated?

7. Can students create their own homework?

8. Does homework have to be by the book, or can students create their own way to demonstrate what they learned? For example, in a geometry class, drawing a floor plan of a dream house using geometry skills might be more effective than a worksheet.

9. What happens if students don't do their required homework? For example, students are assigned a chapter to read in a book, and you designed a lesson around the expectation that they had read it. What do you do about the planned lesson?

10. If homework doesn't really count and it isn't corrected by teachers, why is it assigned?

Companion Website

FEBRUARY

Classroom and Behavior Management Issues

Key Question: What are appropriate rewards for students?

Directions: Think about this list and decide how rewards should be implemented in the classroom. It is important to find appropriate rewards. Discuss this topic with your mentor.

Elementary Rewards	Secondary Rewards	
Free time	Free time	
Watch a video	Read a magazine	
Do errands for the teacher	Work on computer	
Lead the line	See a film/video	
Go to the reading center	Food	
Pick out a book	Class trip	
Play with the pet in class	Play sports during day	
Listen to music in class	Listen to music in class	
Stickers	Wear a hat in class	
Pencils	Use the video camera	
Ice cream	Time off from school	
A certificate	Be coach's assistant	
Pizza party	Make a T-shirt	
Magic markers	Teach a class	
Free recess	Free homework pass	
Sit next to a friend for a day	Read a newspaper	

Companion Website

Looking at Student Work Together

Key Question: How can identifying one key skill enhance student learning?

Directions: By looking at student work with your mentor, you learn what students need to move to the next level of learning. Bring four work samples that are below standard to a meeting. Ask your mentor to help you find one skill for each student that would be the next thing this student should learn. Taking underperforming learners and moving them step-by-step allows the student to feel some level of success. It also clearly identifies one skill to focus on. Ask yourself, what should the student learn next that is developmentally appropriate? How can that one skill be a tipping point for more learning? Discuss any patterns or trends that emerge with all four students.

Student	List several skills student is not meeting	What is the one skill the student could focus on next to improve learning
1.		
2.		
3.		
4.		

Companion Website

Communicating With Parents

Key Question: How could you update parents about content?

Directions: Review this process with your mentor and try this or another idea that will support this concept.

Monthly Content Updates

Parents need to know what the students are learning so that when novice teachers contact them, they understand how they can be helpful at home. Parents can also be valuable partners to teaching if they are familiar with the topic and have experience speaking in classrooms. Use the update as a way to get volunteers, guest speakers, and even some donations! Elementary teachers may use this model, and secondary teachers would focus on their content and list units of study.

Content Update for February Ms. Smith Grade 5		
Content Areas	**What We Are Learning**	**How You Can Help Us Learn . . .**
Math	Fractions	Donate some manipulates we can use. Come to class as a volunteer to tutor students.
Science	Ecology unit (saving our rivers)	Be a guest speaker. Allow us to visit you at your work (i.e., field trip).
Social Studies	World War II	Be a guest speaker (you know about the war or a grandparent may have served in the war).
Language Arts	Writing letters	Share your letter writing skills and sample letters you have written. Donate stationery, stamps, or pens so the class can write real letters to people in a nursing home.

Add at the end of the memo to Contact Ms. Smith at 552-XXXX if you can help our class this month. Thank you!

February Novice Teacher Reflections

Directions: Complete any of these prompts to summarize your experience this month, or add your own. Compare and share your reflections with your mentor or other novice teachers in your support group. You can also reflect on these prompts in your Novice Teacher Journal.

I am still working on . . .

My biggest challenge is . . .

One thing I could do for fun . . .

As a 2+ year teacher I am learning . . .

My students are . . .

Using Mindfulness to Explore Teaching Dilemmas

Teaching is complex, and often there are not clear answers to situations that arise while you are being mentored. The teaching dilemmas introduced at the end of each month in the REFLECT section may not always apply to you; however, the process of reflecting on this dilemma will help you think about what you might do if this did happen to you. Sometimes when a situation arises that we didn't anticipate, we react and say things before we think. This journal process will allow you to pause and think about what you would like to say next. These dilemmas are useful for mentoring conversation starters, novice teacher support group discussions, and personal reflection.

Dilemma 7: Is This Content Accurate?

It is February, and it is time for state content tests. The focus on the content this year is very important at your school because the school is under performing. You are a bit uncertain about the history content, and your mentor is coming to observe. You go over the content with the department chair to be sure your information is correct before teaching the lesson. Your mentor is not a history major, so you can't ask him to help you. Your mentor asks you about the content at the end of the lesson. *What do you say?*

Respond to these prompts in your *Novice Teacher Journal*, available on the companion website.

1. State the dilemma as clearly as possible in one sentence if you can.

2. What decision do you need to make in regard to this situation?

3. Write about the emotions that come up for you that relate to this situation. If you have two choices, write how the emotions might be different.

4. Stop and reread what you have written. Underline any key words or phrases that stand out for you.

5. Soften your eyes or close them and take three deep breaths. Ask yourself, what am I missing that I have not noticed. Write that down in your journal.

6. What will you say to yourself? Write your reflection in your journal.

7. If you are truly stuck, bring your dilemma to your lead mentor, a mentor support group meeting, or to another experienced mentor. Ask him or her to listen to what you have written and to ask you questions to clarify your dilemma. *Your lead mentor's role is not to tell you what to do! No advice!* Just questions to help you clarify what you want to do.

8. After you have spoken to a mentor, write his reaction and how you feel about this dilemma now. All dilemmas are not resolved! This is a process of clarifying and understanding how you feel and how you could respond.

Directions: Complete the goal-setting processes alone or with your mentor. Write your responses on this page or in your Novice Teacher Journal, available on the companion website.

1. *Goal for Improving Your Teaching Practices*

   - Review the PLAN–CONNECT–ACT–REFLECT pages you completed in this chapter with your mentor. Look ahead to the March ACTs to see what you may focus on to continue your development.

   - Acknowledge what you are learning. Be specific! Compliment yourself for doing something well!

   - Reflect on your teaching this month. What stood out as effective? What will you do differently next month?

   - Agree on ONE goal with your mentor to reinforce your learning for next month.

   - Goal:

VIDEO 2.15

Managing Your Stress

2. *Goal to Support Your Social and Emotional Well-Being*

   - Discuss any challenges you may be facing right now. Challenges often bring stress.

   - Don't ignore any signs of stress! Pay attention and learn ways to manage your stress. Using mindfulness practices can help reduce stress. To learn more about mindfulness and managing stress, watch Video 2.15, *Managing Your Stress*, and read HelpGuide.org's "Benefits of Mindfulness" page and discuss it together. Both are available on the companion website.

   - Goal:

FEBRUARY

> "
> In my opinion, a good teacher is someone who teaches you what you need to know for everyday life and has fun doing it.
>
> —EIGHTH-GRADE STUDENT

NOVICE TEACHER PHASE: COLLEGIALITY

"I want to improve my practice. Can you help me?"

NOVICE TEACHER AFFIRMATION

I am empowered to solve my daily challenges.

MARCH

COLLABORATING WITH YOUR MENTOR

Building a Trusting Relationship

GUIDING QUESTIONS

1. How do I reflect and improve my teaching practices? The **Collaborate ACTivities** section will provide you with options to discuss with your mentor.

2. How will I keep students central to my mentoring conversations? Use the **Student ACTivities** to revisit these topics.

3. Why is it important to reach out to the community and business partners? Use the **Communicate ACTivity** as a way to introduce this topic.

Interstate Teacher Assessment and Support Consortium—InTASC Standards

Review InTASC Standard 10.

- **Standard 10 Leadership and Collaboration**

The teacher seeks appropriate leadership roles and opportunities to take responsibility for student learning, to collaborate with learners, families, colleagues, other school professionals, and community members to ensure learner growth, and to advance the profession.

Chapter Overview

Collaboration can be fun. Teaching has often been called an isolating profession, and many people think it is still that way. Today, there are more opportunities to co-teach, create curriculum together, work across disciplines, and create teacher study groups. Collaboration can also be challenging work. It means meetings, discussions, and decisions based on input from more than one person. Some teachers think it just isn't worth it. Others have made it enjoyable and a refreshing departure from a day spent mostly with students. Discuss collegiality and professionalism with your mentor. Discuss collegiality and professionalism with other novice teachers with whom you work.

The quote from the student on the title page for this month lets you know that students notice when teachers are having fun teaching. It makes a difference if you present a lesson that you really feel passionate about. What do you like to teach? How do the students know you like it?

InTASC Principle 10 Leadership and Collaboration highlights the importance of leadership roles in the school. Novice teachers can be leaders, too. Your mentor can help you take on small leadership roles in the school. Watch the *Sharing Best Practices: Emerging Teacher Leaders* video, available on the companion website, with your mentor and see if you would like to collaborate to organize a support group for beginning teachers.

Follow the PLAN, CONNECT, ACT, REFLECT, and SET GOALS sections in this chapter to guide your mentoring conversations and reflections. Watch and listen to a mentor share her insights in Video 2.16, *Mentoring in Action: March Chapter Introduction*, on the companion website or scan the QR code on a mobile device.

VIDEO 2.16

Mentoring in Action: March Chapter Introduction

MARCH

Novice Teacher Journal

One way to plan your month is to assess where you are right now. Writing in your Novice Teacher Journal will help you document what you are feeling and how to focus your teaching. A digital version of the journal is available on the companion website.

Directions: Review the chapter cover page and the overview for this month. How do this month's topic, the quotes, phase, and affirmation relate to you right now? How are you feeling as you prepare for the school year to begin? What do you feel confident about? Where do you need some help?

Use your journal to record your thoughts, feelings, and questions in a free-flowing narrative. This page is for your personal reflection; it does not need to be shared with your mentor unless you choose to do so. At the end of the year, you can review your monthly reflections to see how much you have grown.

March Entry Date_____

Today I feel . . .

_____

_____

_____

I am confident in the areas of . . .

_____

_____

_____

I need some help . . .

_____

_____

_____

Companion Website

Questions for Participating in Mentoring Conversations

Sometimes you don't know what to ask your mentor because you don't know what you don't know! Review this list and choose some questions that are useful to you. How will your mentor respond? Will you schedule a face-to-face meeting, or a phone appointment, or send an e-mail? What works best for both of you? Reflect on your mentor's responses and think about what works for you. If you are a 2+ year teacher, these may not all apply to you; however, there may be a question you would like to revisit.

Your Possible Questions

- How do I get to know the other teachers in the school?
- What are some of the local agencies I should be aware of that can assist me with students or that offer resources for teachers?
- I would like to sponsor some kind of parent event in my classroom. Can you help me navigate school politics to do that?
- What else do I need to know about relationships in this school that will assist me with my students?

Other questions I have . . .

Anticipate Your Mentor's Questions

- How can I help you connect with other novice teachers in the school or district?
- How are you getting along with other teachers right now?
- What is your next step in connecting with parents?
- What can I do to assist you right now that would help you?

Meetings and Observations

Plan brief weekly meetings with your mentor. The ACTs in this chapter serve as mentoring conversation starters and can also be used to assess or review what you may already know about a given topic.

Plan to meet at times that allow you to have quality time together in a place without interruptions. Use this calendar to schedule your meetings and classroom visits to ensure they will happen! Include watching videos or reading pages in *The First Years Matter* as part of your *PLAN*. A digital version of this calendar (March Calendar.pdf) is available on the companion website.

Self-assess your lessons regularly to note your effectiveness in the classroom. Review the InTASC or district evaluation standards to see if you would rate yourself as proficient. Share your self-assessments with your mentor.

March Calendar

MONDAY	TUESDAY	WEDNESDAY	THURSDAY	FRIDAY

Use this calendar to PLAN the month with your mentor as well as to document meetings.

CONNECT to Additional Resources

CONNECT to School and District Resources

What resources exist in your school and community that could assist you in March?

CONNECT With Colleagues, Parents, and Families

How can you collaborate with members of the school and community?

How are parents and families part of collaboration in your school?

CONNECT to Student Voices

One way to create a positive community is to encourage student compliments. Their voices will model respect and demonstrate verbally how they show respect. Discuss with your mentor how compliments can be integrated into the daily routine. You can model this process by saying, "I would like to compliment John for helping Sarah with her homework yesterday." Compliments should always relate to learning or respectful behavior for the classroom.

CONNECT to Education Hot Topics

Interact with Colleagues! Collaboration is often listed as an important teacher skill. Check out "5 Ways to Get More Out of Teacher-to-Teacher Collaboration" posted on the We Are Teachers website. Sometimes collaboration is difficult. Discuss with your mentor what to do when you have to engage in a hard conversation and check out the featured book on the companion website to help you.

CONNECT With the Companion Website

Video links, forms for this chapter, a featured Corwin author, and other resources by the author are located at resources.corwin.com/mentoringinaction.

The First ACT!

Differentiating Mentoring Conversations

Teaching is complex work, and you can easily become overwhelmed. It is appropriate to customize your mentoring conversations, so your mentor is responding to your needs and skills.

Directions: Discuss the prompts with your mentor or think about them on your own. Refer to your state or district teaching standards to note a common language for teaching and summarize your key ideas in each box. Skim the ACTs for this month and decide which topics are most relevant to your needs this month.

Name_____ Date _____

Monthly Needs Assessment

1. What is going well in your classroom right now?	3. What would you like to improve or enhance in your practice this month?
2. How do you know your practice is working? What is your evidence of success?	4. Review the ACT overview of possible conversations for this month with your mentor. What would you like to focus on this month?

A digital version of this template (Monthly Needs Assessment Sample With Standards.pdf) is available on the companion website. Keep a copy of this assessment in your professional file.

MARCH

Overview of the ACTs for March Conversations

Directions: Skim the ACTivities listed here and complete the pages that will forward your learning. If you are a 2+ year teacher, revisit any ACTs you already completed or try some new ACTs to stretch your thinking. Digital copies of some of the ACTs are available on the companion website.

Key Question Topic	ACTivities	PAGE
Collaborate	ACT 1 **Ways to Receive Feedback**	183
Collaborate	ACT 2 **Observation Options**	184
Collaborate	ACT 3 **Preconference Is a Must**	185
Collaborate	ACT 4 **Observation Feedback Form**	186
Collaborate	ACT 5 **Preparing for a Principal Observation**	187
Students	ACT 6 **Classroom and Behavior Management Issues**	188
Students	ACT 7 **Looking at Student Work Together**	189
Communication	ACT 8 **Communicating With Parents**	190

MARCH

Ways to Receive Feedback

Key Question: How will you receive feedback from your mentor?

Directions: Novice teachers want feedback so they know how to improve. They like praise, but they need specific direction to continue practices that actually have an impact on student learning. Sometimes novice teachers have shared that they don't know what they are doing right because they spend so much time seeing what is wrong. Respectful feedback from your mentor that relates to standards will allow you to grow. This feedback should be data driven and not simply advice. Ask your mentor to provide you with feedback.

Before receiving feedback, you need to reflect on your own experiences and think about how feedback influences you. How does feedback make you feel? What types of feedback are useful to you? Do you like written feedback, so you can think about it later? Do you prefer to have an informal conversation or a formal sit down meeting with your mentor? Your reflections will provide a lens through which to understand how you will feel when your mentor starts to give you feedback. The key is to *ask* your mentor to share with you how she will be giving your feedback. You may also share how you would prefer to receive feedback. These are a variety of ways you may receive feedback. Discuss which ones work best for you.

	Verbal	**Written**
Informal Unplanned	• Talking after a lesson • Seeing each other in the hallway • A five-minute compliment meeting (see Appendix)	• A written note put into the teacher's mailbox
Informal Planned	• Any meetings from Appendix for ten, fifteen, twenty, thirty minutes • Audiotaping a lesson and listening together	• A dialogue journal that you and your mentor keep
Formal Planned	• A mentoring conversation • A formal observation • Videotaping a lesson and discussing	• Data collected at formal observations

Companion Website

Observation Options

Key Question: What are your options for being observed by your mentor?

Directions: Decide together which strategy your mentor will use to gather data about your teaching. Use any of the techniques on this page or create a process of your own. Be sure you understand how each process works; then you will know what your mentor is doing. Set a goal for the observation. What do you want your mentor to observe that will help you be a more effective teacher?

1. *Scripting.* Writing what you say and how you move during the lesson. This is a profile of the lesson in narrative form.

2. *Verbal Feedback.* Listening to your tone and voice. Noting when you are asking questions, giving praise, using talking time, reprimanding, or calling on students.

3. *Movement.* Recording how you move around the room or how students interact with you.

4. *Timing.* Recording the time you spend introducing the lesson, giving directions, answering questions, doing assignments, and cleaning up. How you pace the lesson.

5. *Audiotaping.* Asking your mentor to tape your voice, so you can both hear your articulation, directions, or any specific aspect of speech.

6. *Videotaping.* Asking your mentor to record a lesson and observe the lesson together.

Preconference Conversation Is a Must

Key Question: Why is a preconference important?

Directions: An observation cycle consists of (l) a preconference, at which the process is discussed; (2) the observation, when the data are collected; and (3) a postconference for discussion and feedback about the lesson. Before formally being observed, discuss these processes with your mentor. In the preconference, you are discussing these ideas so that you understand the observation process.

1. Which observation technique will your mentor use? Why did you choose this technique?

2. Review the standards and share what you would like to focus on. The more focused you are, the easier it will be for your mentor to observe. The two of you can decide which technique may be suited to the lesson and what particular skill you are interested in learning more about.

3. Write a formal lesson plan and have your mentor provide feedback to you about it before she observes the lesson.

4. After the data are collected, you will sit together and discuss one specific thing that would improve your teaching practice. This is the postconference. Make sure you schedule this close to the observation. This is the time to acknowledge what is going well, too.

5. You should also reflect on the experience of being observed. It is stressful to have someone come into your classroom. What went well? What will you prepare differently for the next time?

Observation Feedback Form

Key Question: How will your mentor share the observations in writing?

Directions: Your mentor may use a form similar to this one. Review the form he will be using to be fully aware of what will be observed. These are the key ideas that you will be discussing at the postconference. As you prepare your lesson plan, keep these ideas in mind.

Date: _____ Subject/Grade: _____

Time of lesson: _____ Title: _____

1. Clarity of lesson plan:

2. Student learning objective:

3. Engagement of students during the lesson:

4. Modifications for varying abilities:

5. Standards addressed in the lesson:

6. Assessment:

7. Pacing of the lesson:

8. Other observations:

9. Recommendations: *Your mentor will be making recommendations to improve your practice. Be prepared to hear them and discuss how you can implement these suggestions.*

10. Commendations: *Always discuss what you are doing well. We often just focus on the things you need to change. Make sure you end your postconference discussing what is working.*

Preparing for a Principal Observation

Key Question: How can your mentor prepare you for an evaluation observation?

Directions: Novice teachers often get nervous when they are observed by an evaluator. Review the ideas on this page with your mentor so that she can help you prepare for this high-stakes observation. Ask your mentor to conduct a practice observation and use the same forms the principal will be using. Discuss the following.

Before the Observation . . .

- The purpose of the principal's observation is to assess, not to criticize. The principal can learn a lot about you by observing. This is your time to shine.

- Write the objective of the lesson on the board and how it relates to the school standards. What will the students be learning in this lesson, and why are they learning this? Principals want to see standards.

- Talk to other teachers who have been observed to find out what the format of the observation will be.

- Meet with the administrator in advance to share the lesson plan and find out what will be expected during the observation.

- Plan the lesson completely and be sure that all materials and supplies are in place.

- Organize and clean the classroom so the principal can walk around student desks.

During the Observation . . .

- Be yourself and forget that the principal is in the room (if you can!).

- Remember you are not perfect, and you are willing to learn from feedback during the postconference.

After the Observation . . .

- Write down your thoughts about how the lesson went and what you think could be better.

- Attend the postconference meeting with the principal.

- Listen to the feedback and share your perspective.

- Don't defend your actions; rather, be open to suggestions and new learning.

- After the meeting write, in your journal what you learned about yourself in this process.

- Meet with your mentor and share what you learned.

Classroom and Behavior Management Issues

Key Question: How can you document student meetings?

Directions: Review this conference report format with your mentor and discuss other ways to document meetings you have with students in your classroom. This form is available on the companion website.

Individual Student Conference Reports

If you are having difficulty with one student, meet with the student privately to discuss the issue. Use a conference report like the one on this page to document the conversation and to let the student know that this is a formal meeting. The conference report system provides documentation if further action is required by the teacher.

Conference Report

Student's Name: _____ Date: _____

Reason for Conference:

Summary of Conference:

Next Steps:

Signature of Teacher: _____

Signature of Student: _____

Looking at Student Work Together

Key Question: How can you assess growth over time with one student?

Directions: Select a student in the class who is struggling and bring four work samples (from different assignments) to a meeting with your mentor. Take turns looking at each assignment, using your school rubric and assess which skills the student is not meeting for each assignment. Notice if there is a pattern or trend in this student's errors.

Then decide what is one thing you could do to help this student improve. Is the student making the same error on each assignment? Specifically, what does the teacher have to teach this student to move her to the next level?

Assignment Topic	List several skills student is not meeting.	What is ONE skill to focus on that would improve the quality of this assignment?	What does the novice teacher need to do to move the student to the next level of learning?
1.			
2.			
3.			
4.			

Companion Website

Communicating With Parents

Key Question: How can you collaborate with parents and the community?

Directions: There are a variety of ways in which novice teachers can collaborate with parents and other adults in the community. If the school or district has a formal program for community collaboration, use that information to get you started. Discuss the ideas below with your mentor and consider collaborating to organize one of these events.

1. Parent Workshop or Lecture Night

Invite a parent or community member to speak at an evening event held at the school. Select a topic that relates to the content that is being taught this month. The purpose of the event is for the parents to learn the content; then they can either help their children at home or just have a better understanding of what their children are learning in school. Students come to the event with their parents and participate in the workshop or listen to the lecture together. An example of an elementary or middle school workshop could be a hands-on math night where the teacher uses manipulatives to teach fractions. A secondary lecture on an historic event related to a history course or a science lecture related to the science curriculum could be fun for both parents and students. Perhaps the students could be part of the workshop or lecture where they introduce the guest speaker or share some of the work they have done on the topic.

2. Business Partnerships

Mentors from local business may be interested in tutoring or reading to students. By using the adult human resources, novice teachers get to know who is who in the community while also getting some help for their classroom. The partnerships could also provide guest speakers for in school talks or lecture nights. There is also the possibility of donations of older computers and file cabinets that businesses often toss when they are updating and redesigning. Do you have any business connections?

3. Alumni Mentoring Program

Graduates of local high schools and colleges often like to come back to mentor students at risk. Students who have successfully completed a college program often want to give back and pay it forward with students at their school. These young role models show the students that there is a reason to stay in school and get good grades. Graduating from high school is important today, and the dropout rate is growing because of failure on high-stakes tests. Mentoring may help, and it can begin early. How could this idea support you?

March Novice Teacher Reflections

Directions: Complete any of these prompts to summarize your experience this month, or add your own. Compare and share your reflections with your mentor or other novice teachers in your support group. You can also reflect on these prompts in your Novice Teacher Journal.

The best thing that happened this month is . . .

What has helped me the most this year is . . .

Something I would like to see my mentor teach is . . .

As a 2+ year teacher, I am learning . . .

I would like to _____ with my mentor . . .

Using Mindfulness to Explore Teaching Dilemmas

Teaching is complex, and often there are not clear answers to situations that arise while you are being mentored. The teaching dilemmas introduced at the end of each month in the REFLECT section may not always apply to you; however, the process of reflecting on this dilemma will help you think about what you might do if this did happen to you. Sometimes when a situation arises that we didn't anticipate, we react and say things before we think. This journal process will allow you to pause and think about what you would like to say next. These dilemmas are useful for mentoring conversation starters, novice teacher support group discussions, and personal reflection.

Dilemma 8: Being Mentored and Evaluated

March's topic is about collaboration and being observed by your mentor. You have built a wonderful trusting relationship with your mentor and you willingly invite him to your classroom. At this time of year, the principal is also coming to observe and provide feedback to you. The principal is new to your school, and you heard through the grapevine that she has asked your mentor to share what she is seeing when she observes your teaching. You had a few issues in your classroom that you discussed with your mentor and that you don't want the principal to hear about. You need to keep your job, and you don't want the principal looking for evidence that could be used to not renew your contract. You thought the mentor was supposed to be a confidential colleague, and that is why you opened up to her. If she shares this information, you feel that you cannot trust her with any other issues in the future. *What do you do?*

Respond to these prompts in your Novice Teacher journal, available on the companion website.

1. State the dilemma as clearly as possible in one sentence if you can.

2. What decision do you need to make in regard to this situation?

3. Write about the emotions that come up for you that relate to this situation. If you have two choices, write how the emotions might be different.

4. Stop and reread what you have written. Underline any key words or phrases that stand out for you.

5. Soften your eyes or close them and take three deep breaths. Ask yourself, what am I missing that I have not noticed. Write that down in your journal.

6. How can your mentor help you? Write your reflection in your journal.

7. If you are truly stuck, bring your dilemma to another novice teacher who is in his or her second or third year of teaching. Ask him or her to listen and to ask you questions to clarify your dilemma. Ask her not to give advice, just to ask you questions to help you clarify your feelings and next steps.

8. How do you feel about this dilemma now? All dilemmas are not resolved! This is a process of clarifying and understanding how you feel and how you might proceed in the future.

Directions: Complete the goal-setting processes alone or with your mentor. Write your responses on this page or in your Novice Teacher Journal, available on the companion website.

1. *Goal for Improving Your Teaching Practices*

   - Review the PLAN–CONNECT–ACT–REFLECT pages you completed in this chapter with your mentor. Look ahead to the April ACTs to see what you may focus on to continue your development.

   - Acknowledge what you are learning. What showed up in your observations as commendations?

   - Reflect on your teaching this month. What stood out as effective? What will you do differently next month?

   - Agree on ONE goal with your mentor to reinforce for next month.

   - Goal:

2. *Goal to Support Your Social and Emotional Well-Being*

   - Discuss any challenges you may be facing right now. Challenges often bring stress.

   - Don't ignore any signs of stress! Pay attention and learn ways to manage stress.

   - Explore mindfulness and Jon Kabat-Zinn's work. Select any one of his YouTube videos to learn more ways to reduce stress and promote wellness.

   - Goal:

MARCH

> **"**
> A good teacher goes to teacher school.
> —FIRST-GRADE STUDENT

NOVICE TEACHER PHASE: CONFUSION

"How can I teach what is important and also meet the district standards for high-stakes tests?"

NOVICE TEACHER AFFIRMATION

I am a mindful teacher who focuses my mentoring conversations on student learning.

APRIL

STANDARDS

Creating Meaningful Standards-Based Learning Experiences for Students

GUIDING QUESTIONS

1. How do I set realistic goals to improve my practice? The **Goals ACTivities** will provide ways to approach this task.

2. How can I use student observation as a way to improve my practice? Use the **Student ACTivities** as a guide.

3. How can I share the importance of good study skills with parents? Use the **Communicate ACTivity** as a discussion starter with your mentor.

Interstate Teacher Assessment and Support Consortium—InTASC Standards

Revisit InTASC Standards 1, 2, and 3.

- **Standard 1 Learner Development**

The teacher understands how learners grow and develop, recognizing that patterns of learning and development vary individually within and across the cognitive, linguistic, social, emotional, and physical areas, and designs and implements developmentally appropriate and challenging learning experiences.

- **Standard 2 Learning Differences**

The teacher uses understanding of individual differences and diverse cultures and communities to ensure inclusive learning environments that enable each learner to meet high standards.

- **Standard 3 Learning Environments**

The teacher works with others to create environments that support individual and collaborative learning, and that encourage positive social interaction, active engagement in learning, and self motivation.

Chapter Overview

The first-grade student who said, "A good teacher goes to teacher school," recognized the importance of teacher learning. Teaching is a lifelong learning profession, and as a beginning teacher, you will quickly learn that you will be adding to your knowledge base continually. There is so much to learn, and it all can't be front-loaded in your teacher preparation program. You may have been prepared in a college of education or perhaps took an alternative route to teaching as a career changer. In either case, whatever you learned will change and expand. Your mentor will differentiate the mentoring conversation to accommodate your needs. To do this you need to share what you already know. Ask for help in the areas where you don't feel competent. You may need summer courses or professional development in areas that you may have missed in teacher preparation.

This chapter focuses on standards because they relate to the high-stakes standardized tests that are used to measure student progress. Effective teaching is tied to tests because student success is measured on tests. The dilemma for novice teachers is how can they teach the content in their classrooms at the appropriate pace so that students will have the knowledge to pass these tests. Novice teachers often ask, do I have to teach to the test to have my students meet the passing rates? Are students supposed to miss art, music, and physical exercise to prepare for these tests? Is there any room in the day for the teacher to teach content that is not on the tests? Where *is* the fun in teaching? Some novice teachers are finding there is a disconnect between the models of learning they were taught in teacher preparation programs and the test-taking focus when they get to their first teaching assignment. Discuss this dilemma with your mentor and ask how she is resolving some of these questions.

The affirmation for this month is, "I am a mindful teacher who focuses mentoring conversations on student learning." By paying attention to the purpose of each interaction and conversation you have with your mentor, you bring focus and direction to your learning. Learning how to teach is a full-time job!

Follow the PLAN, CONNECT, ACT, REFLECT, and SET GOALS sections in this chapter to guide your mentoring conversations and reflections.

Watch and listen to a mentor share her insights in the videos titled *Mentoring in Action: April Chapter Introduction* (Video 2.17, Part 1, and Video 2.18, Part 2), available on the companion website or by scanning the QR code on a mobile device.

VIDEO 2.17

Mentoring in Action: April Chapter Introduction, Part 1

VIDEO 2.18

Mentoring in Action: April Chapter Introduction, Part 2

APRIL

Companion Website

Novice Teacher Journal

One way to plan your month is to assess where you are right now. Writing in your Novice Teacher Journal will help you document what you are feeling and how to focus your teaching. A digital version of the journal is available on the companion website.

Directions: Review the chapter cover page and the overview for this month. How do this month's topic, the quotes, phase, and affirmation relate to you right now? How are you feeling as you prepare for the school year to begin? What do you feel confident about? Where do you need some help?

Use your journal to record your thoughts, feelings, and questions in a free-flowing narrative. This page is for your personal reflection; it does not need to be shared with your mentor unless you choose to do so. At the end of the year, you can review your monthly reflections to see how much you have grown.

April Entry Date_____

Today I feel . . .

_____

_____

_____

I am confident in the areas of . . .

_____

_____

_____

I need some help . . .

_____

_____

_____

APRIL

Companion Website

Questions for Participating in Mentoring Conversations

Sometimes you don't know what to ask your mentor because you don't know what you don't know! Review this list and choose some questions that are useful to you. If you are a 2+ year teacher, these may not all apply to you; however, there may be a question you would like to revisit.

Your Possible Questions

1. Can you review with me how to make content meaningful?

2. My students seem to be changing at this time of year. I need help remembering my adolescent and child psychology. Is this supposed to be happening, or are my students different?

3. The diversity in my room is overwhelming. I have so many learning styles. What can I do?

4. Instructional strategies for diverse learners are important, but I find myself teaching the whole class the same way. Do you have any suggestions?

5. The behavior in my room is really challenging. I need a refresher. Are there any support systems for me right now?

6. I am trying to communicate in different ways with my students. Can you review them with me to be sure I am on track?

7. I don't have time to plan the way I did in the fall. I know that when I do, the day goes much better, but I just can't fit everything in. Can you help me get organized?

Other questions I have . . .

Anticipate Your Mentor's Questions

1. What can I do to assist you right now that would reduce your anxiety?

2. How are you preparing for your lessons?

3. What are you doing to balance your teaching and personal life?

APRIL

Meetings and Observations

Plan brief weekly meetings with your mentor. The ACTs in this chapter serve as mentoring conversation starters and can also be used to assess or review what you may already know about a given topic.

Plan to meet at times that allow you to have quality time together in a place without interruptions. Knowing when you will meet each week reduces anxiety for you. You will find that you look forward to regularly scheduled meetings especially if they are short. Use this calendar to document your meetings and invite your mentor to schedule classroom visits to see you in action. There are many videos in this book and also in your mentor's *Mentoring in Action* book. Consider scheduling time to watch the videos together and have a discussion. A digital version of this calendar (April Calendar.pdf) is available on the companion website.

In April, many districts have to make a decision about rehiring. If your evaluator from the district has not yet observed you teach it may happen this month. Practice the observation cycle with your mentor and ask her to role play the principal. Review the evaluation standards and any pages in this book that can support you in demonstrating proficiency on your evaluation.

April Calendar

MONDAY	TUESDAY	WEDNESDAY	THURSDAY	FRIDAY

Use this calendar to PLAN the month with your mentor as well as to document meetings and observations.

Companion Website

CONNECT to Additional Resources

CONNECT to School and District Resources

What resources exist in your school and community that could assist you in April?

CONNECT With Colleagues, Parents, and Families

Who can help you understand standards-based learning in your school?

How can parents be helpful in supporting you with testing?

CONNECT to Student Voices

Personally interview students who are showing recurring misbehavior in the classroom. Come from a place of respect and tell the student that these behaviors are not acceptable but also share how to change the behavior. These personal conferences allow you to look into the student's eyes. Questions to consider are (1) Why are you behaving this way in the classroom? and (2) How can I help you? By taking the time to meet alone, the student's voice can be heard.

CONNECT to Education Hot Topics

Exercise, Sleep, and Diet. You may find yourself exhausted at this point in the year. Find ways to "move" and stand up and stretch or take a walk around the building when you feel stressed or tired. Have a "walk and talk" mentor conversation instead of sitting. Go home and sleep for at least eight hours for at least one night! Eat a healthy snack!

CONNECT With the Companion Website

Video links, forms for this chapter, a featured book, and other resources by the author are located at resources.corwin.com/mentoringinaction.

APRIL

The First ACT!

Differentiating Mentoring Conversations

Teaching is complex work, and you can easily become overwhelmed. It is appropriate to customize your mentoring conversations so that your mentor is responding to your needs and skills.

Directions: Discuss the prompts with your mentor or think about them on your own. Refer to your state or district teaching standards to note a common language for teaching and summarize your key ideas in each box. Skim the ACTs for this month and decide which topics are most relevant to your needs this month.

Name_____ Date _____

Monthly Needs Assessment

1. What is going well in your classroom right now?	3. What would you like to improve or enhance in your practice this month?
2. How do you know your practice is working? What is your evidence of success?	4. Review the ACT overview of possible conversations for this month with your mentor. What would you like to focus on this month?

A digital version of this template (Monthly Needs Assessment Sample With Standards.pdf) is available on the companion website. Keep a copy of this assessment in your professional file.

Companion Website

Overview of the ACTs for April Conversations

Directions: Skim the ACTivities listed here and complete the pages that will forward your learning. Digital copies of some of the ACTs are available on the companion website.

Key Question Topic	ACTivities	PAGE
Goals	ACT 1 **Novice Teacher Goals**	203
Goals	ACT 2 **Classroom and District Learning Standards**	204
Goals	ACT 3 **Reducing Teacher Talking Time (TTT)**	205
Goals	ACT 4 **Designing Relevant Lessons**	206
Students	ACT 5 **Observing a Student or Small Group**	207
Students	ACT 6 **Classroom and Behavior Management Issues**	208
Students	ACT 7 **Looking at Student Work Together**	209
Communicate	ACT 8 **Communicating With Parents**	210

Novice Teacher Goals

Key Question: How do you review your teaching goals and assess your growth?

Directions: Review your notes, the First ACT pages, your reflections and observations, to assess your growth over time. We know that teaching is a developmental process, and you learn as you teach. Take some time to reflect and decide where you need to focus your mentoring conversations for this final part of the year.

1. What were your goals this year? Have you seen progress toward these goals?

2. What are your three strengths?

3. What two areas should you focus on for the rest of the year?

4. Do you need additional support? (i.e., Do you need to talk with your mentor about unresolved challenges? such as specific students or other issues?)

5. Write a goal with your mentor that will use your strengths to move you forward. Select a goal that encompasses an area that would improve your overall teaching.

Sample goals:

- Motivating introductions to each lesson to settle students and gain attention
- Culminating a lesson in an orderly way that includes a summary and a short informal assessment
- Moving around the classroom more to engage learners
- Pronouncing words correctly and names of students clearly
- Creating efficient routines for collecting papers, passing out materials, collecting homework, and so on

Companion Website

Classroom and District Learning Standards

Key Question: How do you relate district standards to classroom teaching?

Directions: Review the standards and make sure you understand what the students will be required to demonstrate for school or district tests. Lesson plans and curriculum need to stay on track at the end of the year so students have the content required on any tests. Remember that standards are not activities. Many novice teachers get excited about "doing activities" with their students but then have difficulty relating what they are doing to a standard. Ask your mentor to review any of your activities to make sure they align to a standard.

Reflect on your own or review a lesson plan with your mentor using these guiding questions.

1. What is the purpose of this lesson?

2. Why are you teaching this?

3. Why are you teaching it now?

4. Is it part of a larger unit of study?

5. Which standards relate to this lesson?

6. Why did you select them?

7. How do you think students will respond to this lesson?

8. Will all learners be engaged? How will you know?

9. Is there any aspect of your lesson you anticipate may be challenging? Why?

10. What is the most valuable part of this lesson that relates to learning?

APRIL

Reducing Teacher Talking Time (TTT)

Key Question: How can you let students talk more?

Directions: An excellent soccer coach once said that you create good players by giving them as many "touches on the ball" as possible during every practice session. Teachers who talk the whole lesson and never let the students talk or engage in the curriculum are like coaches who tell the players how to do it but never let them practice. How much time are you talking during any lesson, and how much time do you allow the students to talk to each other. Review the ideas on this page with your mentor and integrate more purposeful student talking time into your classroom.

How can you increase purposeful Student Talking Time (STT)?

- Integrate paired sharing into lessons.
- Allow time for discussion in lessons.
- Begin each class with time for students to share what they already know about a topic.
- End a class with time to share what they learned today.
- Partner English language learners with native speakers.
- Include read-aloud activities in lessons.
- Add your ideas!

Remember that the talking needs to relate to learning objectives that relate to the standards. Be mindful about what you are teaching and why. Allowing student learners to talk in class is one way to keep them alert and engaged. Just like in soccer, players who are on the field have to be engaged. The students won't be bored and are less likely to misbehave if they are "playing" in the game.

Companion Website

Designing Relevant Lessons

Key Question: How can you connect the standards to real life activities?

Directions: Service learning engages students and makes the curriculum come alive for all learners. Service projects are offered to the community as a way for students to contribute and learn how to be good citizens. These projects can be part of the existing curriculum or offered as enrichment, extra credit, and homework for those students who are committed to make a difference. You can connect to the community and make the standards come alive for your students. Find ways to motivate the unmotivated students in participating in "service learning" in the community. Review the ideas below and discuss what the students would have to demonstrate as a result of doing this service. Ask your mentor for other ideas.

Add the standard that is met by participating in this service activity.

History, middle/high	Interview and audiotape World War II veterans; then have them come to the classroom as guest speakers. Provide a service to the local veteran's association as part of this activity. Standard:
Science, middle/high	Connect with a recycling center on a project that relates to the science chapter on recycling. Standard:
Elementary	Write to the elderly and visit them on holidays; use as language arts standard. Standard:
Elementary, middle, high	Volunteer at a shelter or soup kitchen and write about the experience. Standards:
Elementary	Invite local businesses into the classroom while learning about professions and select one that needs a special project completed. Standard:

Companion Website

APRIL

Observing a Student or Small Group

Key Question: How can you observe your own students to learn about your teaching?

Directions: At this time of year, there is often at least one student who is still challenging you. This process allows you to step back and observe how the student is interacting in the classroom. If there is not one challenging student, then observe a small group to notice the dynamics when students interact.

Ask your mentor to teach a lesson in your classroom; then you can observe your students. Observe your most challenging student or a small group, whichever option you decide to do. Be clinical in your observation using the data collection form below. Think like an ethnographer who is observing to gather data. The exercise may bring you a new perspective that may assist you in working with this student differently for the rest of the year.

1. First Name of Student: _____ Date of Observation: _____

    - What do you notice about this student (physical appearance, cultural background, language, social interaction, skills and abilities, motivation, attitude, self-concept, etc.)?

    - How is the student responding to the teacher's lesson?

    - Is the student interacting with any other students? Describe.

    - What is the quality of the student's work?

    - Name something positive the student did during the lesson.

    - What other things did you observe that you didn't know about the student?

    - How will this observation help you teach differently? Discuss with your mentor.

2. Small Group Members _____ Date of Observation: _____

    Novice teachers are encouraged to group their students to enhance learning, but often grouping students creates behavior problems. So what is a teacher to do? Not grouping leaves students bored and teachers doing all the talking, yet grouping may be too challenging. Observe a small group in action and see what works and what doesn't. All group work should relate to a curriculum standard and not just be busy work.

    - Why is this small group working together?

    - Who is the leader of the group? Self-appointed or teacher-appointed?

    - How effective is the leader?

    - Is the group completing the assigned task? How do you know?

    - Are all members of the group participating?

    - What are the differences in the individual members' contributions to the group? Give an example.

    - What is your overall impression of this group activity?

    - What did you learn about group dynamics? Discuss with your mentor.

Companion Website

Classroom and Behavior Management Issues

Key Question: How can you document changes in student behavior?

Directions: At this time of the year, students will be testing your patience and skills. Sometimes it helps to have the student state in writing how he or she will change the behavior that has been so disruptive. Here is a model. The key here is having the students write how their success will be measured. How will you know the student has changed? Also, the reward is important, and the teacher should add a by when _____ (date) or else the reward expires! Discuss this process with your mentor to create a system for improving behavior. This form is available on the companion website.

Student Contract

I state that I will (*change a certain behavior*)

_____

_____

_____

I will measure my success by (*how the behavior will be noted as being done*)

_____

_____

_____

For successful demonstration (*I will receive a reward*)

_____

_____

_____

Signed (teacher)_____ Date _____

Signed (student) _____ Date _____

The contract can also be designed for groups by changing *I* to *we*.

Looking at Student Work Together

Key Question: How can you focus on seeing one good thing in student work?

Directions: What are the students doing right even if they are below standard? Bring a variety of work samples to a meeting. After the samples have been sorted into one of the three standards categories (or your own categories), select one sample from each pile. Look for one thing that this student can be complimented for on this paper. Discuss why complimenting students is important to improving progress.

Below Standard	Meets the Standard	Above Standard
How many papers here?	How many papers here?	How many papers here?
% of class _____	% of class _____	% of class _____
Select ONE paper:	Select ONE paper:	Select ONE paper:
What can this student be complimented for?	What can this student be complimented for?	What can this student be complimented for?

Companion Website

Communicating With Parents

Key Question: How can you educate parents to help with study skills?

Directions: Parents know schoolwork, homework, and tests are important, but they often don't know how to help their children learn. Ask your mentor to share ways you can educate parents to help their children.

1. Offer a parent study skill information night.

2. Create a parent "study guide" to help your children.

3. List the effective skills you would discuss and note the behaviors the parent would see if her child were effectively "studying" at home.

Effective Study Skill	Elementary Students	Secondary Students
What is it? Describe the skill.	What behavior would parent see?	What behavior would parent see?
Homework paper		
Studying for a test		
Reading a chapter and taking notes		

Companion Website

April Novice Teacher Reflections

Directions: Complete any of these prompts to summarize your experience this month, or add your own. Compare and share your reflections with your mentor and consider using them as evidence of reflection for teacher evaluation.

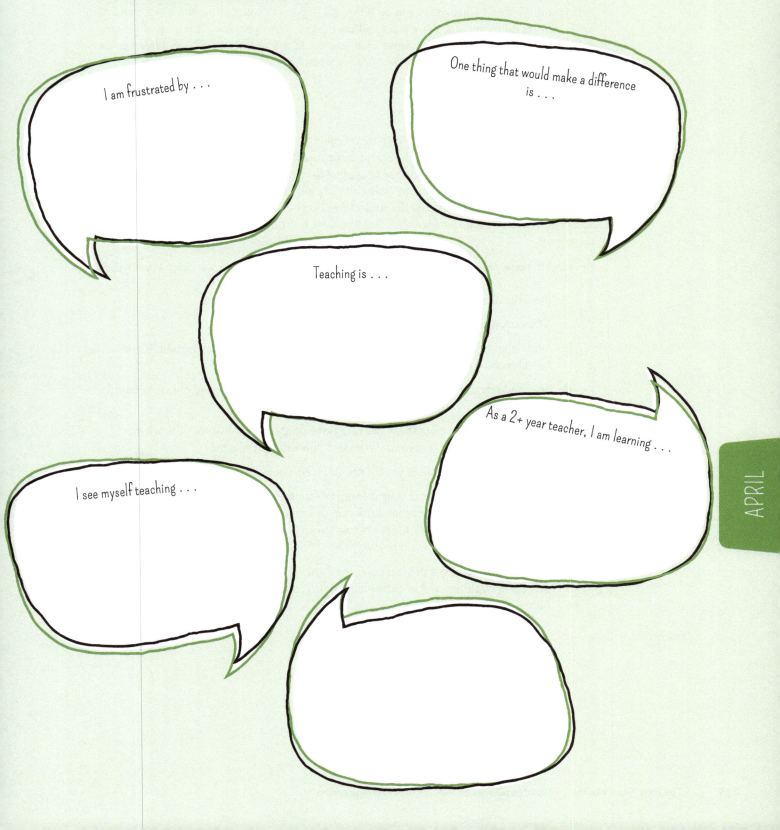

I am frustrated by . . .

One thing that would make a difference is . . .

Teaching is . . .

As a 2+ year teacher, I am learning . . .

I see myself teaching . . .

APRIL

Using Mindfulness to Explore Teaching Dilemmas

Teaching is complex, and often there are not clear answers to situations that arise while you are being mentored. The teaching dilemmas introduced at the end of each month in the REFLECT section may not always apply to you; however, the process of reflecting on this dilemma will help you think about what you might do if this did happen to you. Sometimes when a situation arises that we didn't anticipate, we react and say things before we think. This journal process will allow you to pause and think about what you would like to say next. These dilemmas are useful for mentoring conversation starters, novice teacher support group discussions, and personal reflection.

Dilemma 9: Teaching to the Test

Your district needs higher scores to keep their funding. As a beginning teacher, you are having trouble covering all of the content in time to make sure the students have learned it before the test. You feel nervous about this and are struggling to engage the students and teach the content at the same time. You feel like you are doing all the right things, and you don't want to just lecture to get through the content because the students will get bored. It is just taking you longer to teach all of the content. You are worried that all the content won't be covered before the test date. *What do you do?*

Respond to these prompts in your Novice Teacher Journal, available on the companion website.

1. State the dilemma as clearly as possible in one sentence if you can.

2. What decision do you need to make in regard to this situation?

3. Write about the emotions that come up for you that relate to this situation. If you have two choices, write how the emotions might be different.

4. Stop and reread what you have written. Underline any key words or phrases that stand out for you.

5. Soften your eyes or close them and take three deep breaths. Ask yourself, what am I missing that I have not noticed. Write that down in your journal.

6. How can your mentor help you? Write your reflection in your journal.

7. If you are truly stuck bring your dilemma to another novice teacher who is in his or her second or third year of teaching. Ask him or her to listen and to ask you questions to clarify your dilemma. Ask him or her not to give advice, just to ask you questions to help you clarify your feelings and next steps.

8. How do you feel about this dilemma now? All dilemmas are not resolved! This is a process of clarifying and understanding how you feel and how you might proceed in the future.

APRIL

Directions: Complete the goal-setting processes alone or with your mentor. Write your responses on this page or in your Novice Teacher Journal, available on the companion website.

1. *Goal for Improving Your Teaching Practices*

   - Review the PLAN–CONNECT–ACT–REFLECT pages you completed in this chapter with your mentor. Look ahead to January ACTs to see what you may focus on to continue your development.

   - Acknowledge what you are learning. List three things that are going well.

   - Reflect on your teaching this month. What stood out as effective? What will you do differently next month?

   - Agree on ONE goal with your mentor to reinforce for next month.

   - Goal:

2. *Goal to Support Your Social and Emotional Well-Being*

   - Discuss any challenges you may be facing right now. Challenges often bring stress.

   - Don't ignore any signs of stress! Pay attention and learn ways to manage stress.

   - Explore the CARE for Teachers website (care4teachers.org) and *RESET,* a book by Kristen Lee Costa, to learn ways to support yourself.

   - Goal:

APRIL

"

Good teachers listen to their students and care
how their students are doing academically.

—HIGH SCHOOL STUDENT

NOVICE TEACHER PHASE: HOPE

"It looks like my students are passing tests and learning.
Maybe I can do this."

NOVICE TEACHER AFFIRMATION

I use my strengths to teach.

MAY

ASSESSING STUDENTS' PROGRESS

High-Stakes Tests and Teacher Assessment

GUIDING QUESTIONS

1. How do I review my teaching practices? The **Reflect ACTivities** will provide ways to discuss and reflect.

2. How will I review assessments required by the district? The **Assess ACTivities** offer ideas to discuss.

3. How will I continue to include students' perspectives? Use the **Student ACTivities** to focus.

4. Why is it important to reach out to parents? Use the **Communicate ACTivity** as a way to focus on ways to connect with parents and families.

Interstate Teacher Assessment and Support Consortium—InTASC Standards

Revisit InTASC Standard 6.

- **Standard 6 Assessment**

The teacher understands and uses multiple methods of assessment to engage learners in their own growth, to monitor learner progress, and to guide the teacher's and learner's decision making.

Chapter Overview

"Good teachers care about how their students are doing academically," says the high school student on the opening page of this chapter. CARE is an important word. How do you express caring to your students? Teachers who are trying to help students learn, as opposed to just giving tests and recording scores, build relationships with students. How are you doing in the "caring" department at this time of year? Do you care about your students and want them to succeed in school and life? Do you carry a sense of respect into the classroom?

The end of the year can be very stressful, but it is also a time for hope. The year is almost over and maybe you did actually teach something! The novice teacher phase for this month is hope. When students demonstrate their learning many novices see that they *can* teach after all. Novice teacher phases go up and down all year. It is important to notice if you are in an upward phase at this point in the year. By having a sense of hope, you are demonstrating success and a willingness to return to the classroom next year. If you are still disillusioned and feeling discouraged with teaching, you may need to talk about whether teaching is the right career choice for you. Discuss this with your mentor. Teaching isn't the vocation for everyone.

The InTASC Principle 6 (Assessment) focuses on both formal and informal assessments. High-stakes tests are not the only measure of success. Learning is developmental, and all students do not learn the identified curriculum the year it is listed in the scope and sequence for the school. Discuss with your mentor the options for students who do not learn at the expected rate.

The Affirmation this month is, "I use my strengths to teach." You do have strengths. Focus on them at this time of year to regain your momentum. Keep hope alive!

Follow the PLAN, CONNECT, ACT, REFLECT, and SET GOALS sections in this chapter to guide your mentoring conversations and reflections.

Watch and listen to a mentor share her insights in Video 2.19, *Mentoring in Action: May Chapter Introduction*, on the companion website or scan the QR code on a mobile device.

VIDEO 2.19

Mentoring in Action: May Chapter Introduction

MAY

Companion Website

Novice Teacher Journal

One way to plan your month is to assess where you are right now. Writing in your Novice Teacher Journal will help you document what you are feeling and how to focus your teaching. A digital version of the journal is available on the companion website.

Directions: Review the chapter cover page and the overview for this month. How do this month's topic, the quotes, phase, and affirmation relate to you right now? How are you feeling as you prepare for the school year to begin? What do you feel confident about? Where do you need some help?

Use your journal to record your thoughts, feelings, and questions in a free-flowing narrative. This page is for your personal reflection; it does not need to be shared with your mentor unless you choose to do so. At the end of the year, you can review your monthly reflections to see how much you have grown.

May Entry Date_____

Today I feel . . .

_____

_____

_____

I am confident in the areas of . . .

_____

_____

_____

I need some help . . .

_____

_____

_____

MAY | Assessing Students' Progress   217

Questions for Participating in Mentoring Conversations

Sometimes you don't know what to ask your mentor because you don't know what you don't know! Review this list and choose some questions that are useful to you. How will your mentor respond? Will you schedule a face-to-face meeting, a phone appointment, or send an e-mail? What works best for both of you? Reflect on your mentor's responses and think about what works for you. If you are a 2+ year teacher these may not all apply to you, however there may be a question you would like to revisit.

Your Possible Questions

1. How do I grade these students at the end of the year?

2. High-stakes tests are taking so much time. How do I fit in my teaching?

3. What end-of-the-year assessments do I need to know?

4. How do you think I am doing?

Other questions I have . . .

Anticipate Your Mentor's Questions

1. What do you need to do right now?

2. What paperwork do you need to discuss?

3. What can I do to assist you right now that would help your well-being?

Meetings and Observations

Plan brief weekly meetings with your mentor. The ACTs in this chapter serve as mentoring conversation starters and can also be used to assess or review what you may already know about a given topic.

Plan to meet at times that allow you to have quality time together in a place without interruptions. Use this calendar to schedule your meetings and classroom visits to ensure they will happen! Include watching videos, reading pages in *The First Years Matter* as part of your *PLAN*. A digital version of this calendar (May Calendar.pdf) is available on the companion website.

Review any feedback from formal observations from the administrators in the district. Make sure you understand what is being asked of you and that you can meet these expectations in the classroom. What do you need to do to improve any of your teaching practices? Discuss ACTs with your mentor that will help you.

May Calendar

MONDAY	TUESDAY	WEDNESDAY	THURSDAY	FRIDAY

Use this calendar to PLAN the month with your mentor as well as to document meetings.

Companion Website

CONNECT to Additional Resources

CONNECT to School and District Resources

What resources exist in your school and community that could assist you in May?

CONNECT With Colleagues, Parents, and Families

What district departments relate to assessing student progress and referrals for next year?

How are parents included in end-of-the-year student assessments?

CONNECT to Student Voices

Include informal student self-assessment into your lessons and units. Ask the students to respond to a question during class such as, "Is this work hard or easy." By putting thumbs up or down you will learn if the class understands what you are saying. Try a "ticket" to leave at the end of the class where you ask students to tell you one thing they learned today. Another idea is to use colored cards on the students' desks to indicate green (I am done) and red (I need more time). Ask students to use the appropriate card in response to the question, do you need more time?

CONNECT to Education Hot Topics

Dress code! What is the policy at your school? Are you dressing for success, or have you relaxed your style at the end of the year? Professional dress is always appropriate, and it creates a visual boundary between student and teacher. Dressing like a teacher helps you at the end of the year. One special day of informal dress is okay for fun.

CONNECT on the Corwin Companion Website

Video links, forms for this chapter, a featured Corwin author, and other resources by the author are located at resources.corwin.com/mentoringinaction.

MAY

The First ACT!

Differentiating Mentoring Conversations

Teaching is complex work, and you can easily become overwhelmed. It is appropriate to customize your mentoring conversations to ensure your mentor is responding to your needs and skills.

Directions: Discuss the prompts with your mentor or think about them on your own. Refer to your state or district teaching standards to note a common language for teaching and summarize your key ideas in each box. Skim the ACTS for this month and decide which topics are most relevant to your needs this month.

Name_____ Date _____

Monthly Needs Assessment

1. What is going well in your classroom right now?	3. What would you like to improve or enhance in your practice this month?
2. How do you know your practice is working? What is your evidence of success?	4. Review the ACT overview of possible conversations for this month with your mentor. What would you like to focus on this month?

A digital version of this template (Monthly Needs Assessment Sample With Standards.pdf) is available on the companion website. Keep a copy of this assessment in your professional file.

Companion Website

MAY

Overview of the ACTs for May Conversations

Directions: Skim the ACTivities listed here and complete the pages that will forward your learning. If you are a 2+ year teacher, revisit any ACTs you already completed or try some new ACTs to stretch your thinking. Digital copies of some of the ACTs are available on the companion website.

Key Question Topic	ACTivities	PAGE
Reflect	ACT 1 **Assessing Your Progress**	222
Reflect	ACT 2 **Your Portfolio Assessment**	223
Assess	ACT 3 **Measuring Student Progress**	224
Assess	ACT 4 **Student Self-Assessment of Progress**	225
Assess	ACT 5 **Assessing the Whole Student**	226
Students	ACT 6 **Classroom and Behavior Management Issues**	227
Students	ACT 7 **Looking at Student Work Together**	228
Communicate	ACT 8 **Communicating With Parents**	229

MAY

Assessing Your Progress

Key Question: How are you progressing toward the goal of becoming an effective teacher?

Directions: Reflect on your progress from August until now and rate your performance using a district rubric or the one below. Be clear about the evidence and criteria for success. This does not have to be shared with your mentor; however, if you do share it, she can help you focus your learning for the last month. If you color coded this book to the teacher evaluation standards, review the pages you completed and see if you are missing any target areas. Would you rate yourself as proficient?

Example of Novice Teacher Rubric for Instructional Practice					
	Excellent Progress	**Good Progress**	**Needs More Development**	**Needs Assistance**	**Unsatisfactory**
Demonstrates creativity and thought in planning					
Uses a variety of teaching strategies and methods to engage learners					
Develops both long-form and short-form lesson plans					
Demonstrates principles and theories of instruction for students in the classroom					
Demonstrates proper sequencing and pacing of lessons					
Develops and modifies curriculum to meet student needs					
Manages the classroom					
Handles difficult situations through problem-solving approaches					
Maintains an organized classroom for student learning					
Disciplines fairly					

Companion Website

MAY

Your Portfolio Assessment

Key Question: How can you demonstrate effectiveness using a portfolio?

Directions: A portfolio is a collection of carefully selected artifacts that illustrate the standards that have been completed this year. If you are interested in sharing his skills through this method, select artifacts that align to teacher evaluation standards. Reflecting is a key component to a portfolio. Explain why you select each artifact and how it demonstrates that you are an effective teacher. Discuss these steps with your mentor.

Step 1	Review all materials from this year (i.e., lesson plans, units, etc.). What stands out as interesting, colorful, and meaningful to share with your evaluator and others?
Step 2	Select key items, photos, samples of student work, and notes from parents that, for example, illustrate something the novice teacher wants to share. It could be a standard for teaching, a competency, a skill, or an interest. It could also be related to the InTASC standards listed on the cover sheet of each month in this book. Less is more!
Step 3	Write a short description or caption for each item selected. Describe what it is and why it is in the portfolio.
Step 4	Write a short reflection for each item and place it below the description or caption. The reflection explains what you learned from teaching this, what you would do differently, or something that is an insight for you that relates to this photo or lesson.
Step 5	Lay the artifact, description, and reflection on a page under a TITLE that clearly identifies the message to the reader. If the novice teacher is organizing the portfolio by InTASC standards, perhaps the standard is part of the title.
Step 6	Put all the pages together. Place the Philosophy Statement up front and write a Final Statement for the last page. This Final Statement could include what I learned this year as a first-year teacher, my goals for year 2, and my future aspirations as an educator.

Companion
Website

MAY

Measuring Student Progress

Key Question: What are the types of assessments you should know?

Directions: Ask your mentor to review these three types of assessments: Diagnostic, Formative, and Summative, and to share models of each type of test so you understand the difference. At this time of year, high-stakes tests that measure student progress or graduation standards are also being given. You need to know how the classroom instruction impacts all these assessment results.

1. Diagnostic Assessments
   - Used before instruction begins
   - Capture prior knowledge and skills
   - Test for readiness

2. Formative Assessments
   - Used daily to measure understanding
   - Gauge progress on a skill or lesson activity
   - Incorporate weekly quizzes or tickets to leave

3. Summative Assessments
   - Used at the end of units
   - Used to measure growth
   - Contribute to card grades

4. High-Stakes Tests
   - Benchmarks for district growth
   - Graduation requirements for state
   - Determine merit pay for teachers

Companion
Website

Student Self-Assessment of Progress

Key Question: How can you create a student self-assessment survey?

Directions: Create a student self-assessment survey with your mentor to capture the key questions you want to know from your students. The survey assessment can be general, or if you want to get specific, you can design it that way. Decide whether these surveys should be anonymous or the students should put their names on the papers. Discuss the benefits of either choice.

Sample Questions

1. List something you learned in this class.

2. How would you rate your effort in this class? (1–10)

3. What do you like most about this class?

4. What is your goal after high school?

5. How can teachers help you learn better?

6. Did you do your homework regularly? Why or why not?

7. What do you like most about school?

8. How could you be a better student?

9. How did you do in this course?

10. Does your grade match your effort and work?

MAY

Assessing the Whole Student

Key Question: How can you in see the whole child's progress?

Directions: Think about how you can assess a student's progress in school. Look at multiple measures of growth, not just the summative and high-stakes tests. Observe each student as a whole person, not just the score on a test. Students may have some level of success and learning this year and just don't score well on a test. Broaden your perspective of learning and success. Look at each student through these lenses. Discuss what you learn in this process with your mentor.

1. *Student Personal Strengths*
   - Ability to speak languages
   - Musical ability
   - Hobbies
   - Technology skills
   - Athletic ability
   - Artistic skills
   - Reading
   - Theatre
   - Sports
   - Sense of humor

2. *Interpersonal and Social Interactions*
   - With other students in the classroom
   - In the school helping others
   - Leadership in community groups

3. *Academic Achievement in Classes*
   - On units of study based on teacher-made tests and quizzes (paper and pencil)
   - Project or performance based
   - Performance portfolios

4. *High-Stakes Testing Results*

5. *Other Indicators of Success*

Companion Website

Classroom and Behavior Management Issues

Key Question: What do you need to know about students at the end of the year?

Directions: As the year comes to a close, sometimes student misbehavior escalates. Everyone is tired, and you may have exhausted your good ideas. Review these strategies that were introduced earlier in the year. Which ones might be useful to try now? Discuss any of these with your mentor.

1. Focus on positive behavior when it happens.

   - Give verbal praise for specific behavior.
   - Send notes home with students.
   - Make complimentary phone calls to parents about their child.

2. Don't threaten or bribe students to behave.

   - Students may respond for a short term.
   - Bribes show a sign of weakness in the teacher.
   - The teacher loses respect.

3. Take charge of the classroom in a firm but pleasant manner.

   - Use your sense of humor to keep students in line.
   - Communicate your needs honestly to students.
   - Listen to your students' requests and complaints.

4. Give "I"-messages to students instead of "You"-messages.

   - "I am unhappy with the behavior I am seeing," not "You are misbehaving again."

5. Use body language and signals to prevent disruptive behavior.

   - Make eye contact with the misbehaving student.
   - Use frown or facial expression.
   - Walk near the student and lightly tap his or her shoulder.
   - Use your sense of humor.
   - Use a cue to have the students look at you (e.g., lights off, raise hands).

6. Don't use sarcasm, cruel remarks, or words to embarrass students.

   - No ridicule or intimidation allowed!
   - Never touch a student in an abusive way.
   - Confrontation in front of a whole class is not recommended.
   - If the situation becomes confrontational, remove the student and discuss the problem later.

Looking at Student Work Together

Key Question: What are your beliefs about modifying and differentiating instruction?

Directions: Do you embrace this concept, or are you still confused as to what it means? Some teachers believe there shouldn't be differentiation and that all learners should be treated the same in a same-age-level classroom. What you believe impacts your teaching. What does your mentor believe? Philosophies are personal, but district standards and approaches for student learning are public. This is a complex topic and meeting the needs of diverse learners in a classroom is not easy.

Ask yourself these questions:

What do you believe about modifying student work assignments and differentiating instruction?

How are you doing this in the classroom?

Look at one sample of student work and differentiate the assignment for this student.

Student	Standard level	What student needs to learn next	How the teacher could differentiate to assist the student in learning

MAY

Communicating With Parents

Key Question: How can you communicate information about tests?

Directions: High-stakes tests are here to stay. In many districts, they mean graduation from high school or not. Teacher-made tests are also part of academic progress, and they serve as the grading system for report cards and moving to the next grade. Both tests are critical to students. So how can parents help? Novice teachers need to assist parents in understanding the difference between high-stakes and teacher tests and how they both impact their children. How are you informing parents about high-stakes tests and teacher-made tests?

High-Stakes Tests (state or district)	Teacher-Made Tests (measure of content learned in the classroom)
(For each type of test) List how it is used and how students benefit from this test.	(For each type of test) List how it is used and how students benefit from this test.

Companion Website

MAY

May Novice Teacher Reflections

Directions: Complete any of these prompts to summarize your experience this month. Add your own prompts to the blank stems. Compare and share your reflections with your mentor or other novice teachers in your support group. A digital version is available on the companion website.

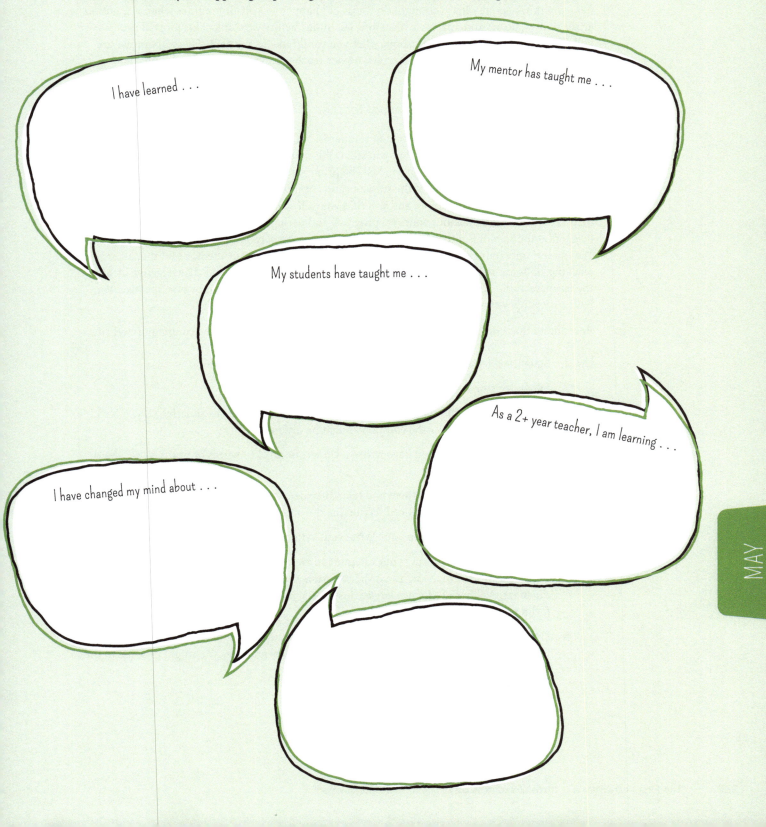

I have learned . . .

My mentor has taught me . . .

My students have taught me . . .

I have changed my mind about . . .

As a 2+ year teacher, I am learning . . .

MAY

Using Mindfulness to Explore Teaching Dilemmas

Teaching is complex, and often there are not clear answers to situations that arise while you are being mentored. The teaching dilemmas introduced at the end of each month in the REFLECT section may not always apply to you; however, the process of reflecting on this dilemma will help you think about what you might do if this did happen to you. Sometimes when a situation arises that we didn't anticipate, we react and say things before we think. This journal process will allow you to pause and think about what you would like to say next. These dilemmas are useful for mentoring conversation starters, novice teacher support group discussions, and personal reflection.

Dilemma 10: Becoming an Effective Teacher

You have seen your growth in all teaching standards. Yet you still feel a bit uneasy about your progress. You are trying your best, but you still think that the context at your school is not helping you be the best teacher you can be. The principal is new and doesn't really know how to give you feedback, and some of the students and parents are challenging you. You wanted to teach, but you have few resources, and you find yourself saying, "I never knew it would be like this!" You feel uncertain about your real progress, and perhaps you might not get rehired. Other teachers at the school feel the same thing, and in the teachers' room, you are agreeing with them. Yet you feel uncertain, and your mentor has been so supportive. Your mentor says that all of your teaching skills are stellar. You do want to stay at the school and be rehired. The negative ideas in the teachers' room seem to agree with what you are feeling, but your mentor is so positive. You have a meeting with your mentor coming up. *What do you say?*

Respond to these prompts in your Novice Teacher Journal, available on the companion website.

1. State the dilemma as clearly as possible in one sentence if you can.

2. What decision do you need to make in regard to this situation?

3. Write about the emotions that come up for you that relate to this situation. If you have two choices, write how the emotions might be different.

4. Stop and reread what you have written. Underline any key words or phrases that stand out for you.

5. Soften your eyes or close them and take three deep breaths. Ask yourself, what am I missing that I have not noticed. Write that down in your journal.

6. How can your mentor help you? Write your reflection in your journal.

7. If you are truly stuck, bring your dilemma to another novice teacher in their second or third year of teaching. Ask him or her to listen and to ask you questions to clarify your dilemma. Ask her not to give advice, just to ask you questions to help you clarify your feelings and next steps.

8. How do you feel about this dilemma now? All dilemmas are not resolved! This is a process of clarifying and understanding how you feel and how you might proceed in the future.

MAY

Directions: Complete the goal-setting processes alone or with your mentor. Write your responses on this page or in your Novice Teacher Journal, available on the companion website.

1. *Goal for Improving Your Teaching Practices*

   - Review the PLAN–CONNECT–ACT–REFLECT pages you completed in this chapter with your mentor. Look ahead to June ACTs to see what you may focus on to continue your development.
   - Acknowledge what you are learning. Find anything to praise!
   - Reflect on your teaching this month. What stood out as effective? What will you do differently next month?
   - Agree on ONE goal with your mentor to reinforce for next month.
   - Goal:

2. *Goal to Support Your Social and Emotional Well-Being*

   - Discuss any challenges you may be facing right now. Challenges often bring stress.
   - Don't ignore any signs of stress! Pay attention and learn ways to manage stress.
   - Explore the CASEL website (casel.org) to learn more ways to promote mindful teaching.
   - Goal:

"

A good teacher adds some humor to teaching.

—SEVENTH-GRADE STUDENT

NOVICE TEACHER PHASE: CELEBRATE, CULMINATE, AND REFLECT

"I felt like I was racing to get everything done for
the last day, and the next day everyone was gone!
No students, no directives from the central office, just me
feeling exhausted and exhilarated. I did it! I finished!
Now I know what I will do differently next year!"

NOVICE TEACHER AFFIRMATION

I am grateful for the opportunity to be
mentored by an experienced teacher.

JUNE

COMPLETING THE YEAR
Paperwork, Relationships, and Closing a Room

GUIDING QUESTIONS

1. How do I reflect on the entire year? The **Reflect ACTivities** will share some options.

2. How will I learn the school closing routines? The **Closing ACTivities** offer you ideas to discuss.

3. How will I keep students in mind at the end of the year? Use the **Student ACTivities** as a way to focus on students.

4. Why is it important to communicate to all parents at the end of the year? Use the **Communicate ACTivity** as a way to think about a final communication.

Interstate Teacher Assessment and Support Consortium—InTASC Standards

Revisit InTASC Standard 9.

- **Standard 9 Professional Learning and Ethical Practice**

The teacher engages in ongoing professional learning and uses evidence to continually evaluate his/her practice, particularly the effects of his/her choices and actions on others (learners, families, other professionals, and the community), and adapts practice to meet the needs of each learner.

Chapter Overview

This is the time to celebrate, culminate the year, and reflect on what you have achieved in one year. It may have felt like a whirlwind so far, and it is not over yet! Don't stop learning from your mentor now. The cleanup and closing down of a classroom take lots of time and energy, and many novice teachers have felt alone doing this task. So stay connected to your mentor at this important time of year.

You have learned so much. You have been guided by an experienced mentor who has shared her ideas and wisdom with you. Humor is an underused emotion in teaching. Take some time to reflect on some of the situations you faced this year and use your humor lens. Yes, it is okay to laugh and be a teacher. Schedule a meeting with your mentor to just discuss the funny things that happened this year. It may take a few minutes, so make an effort to smile, shake your head, and document the crazy things that happen in school with students.

This chapter focuses on nuts and bolts like cleanup and also the more serious side of looking at what actually happened this year. Just like the orientation in August, the ending of the year brings so many little details. Where do the books get stored? Who gets the report cards? How do I lock up and clean up my room? Your mentor has done this many times, so it is second nature, but it may be the first time for you. Take a photo of your classroom before you dismantle it so that you can remember how you want to set it up for next fall.

Use the activities in this chapter to summarize the year and summarize your feelings and emotions. Make time for a few short meetings with your mentor even though the schedules seem packed with other duties. This is the time to celebrate what you have learned. It also is a time to discuss what you will change for next year.

Your Affirmation for this month is, "I am grateful for the opportunity to be mentored by an experienced teacher." If this is your first year in the classroom, you probably had a steep learning curve. If this is your second or third year, you hopefully learned some new things that were helpful.

Your year being mentored is coming to a close. Review your August reflections in your Novice Teacher Journal and reflect on your personal development. Acknowledge yourself for being a teacher. Celebrate your successes this year.

As you have learned this year, teaching takes time and commitment. This chapter will guide you as you think about ways to continue to enhance your teaching. Being grateful that you had an opportunity to be mentored acknowledges and honors what you have learned this year. If you are a 2+ year teacher using this book to deepen your reflection and teaching, think about how the time you have taken for yourself has helped you this year. And watch the videos titled *Mentoring in Action: June Chapter Introduction* (Video 2.20, Part 1, and Video 2.21, Part 2), available on the companion website or by scanning the QR codes on a mobile device.

VIDEO 2.20

Mentoring in Action: June Chapter Introduction, Part 1

VIDEO 2.21

Mentoring in Action: June Chapter Introduction, Part 2

JUNE

Companion Website

Novice Teacher Journal

One way to plan your month is to assess where you are right now. Writing in your Novice Teacher Journal will help you document what you are feeling and how to focus your teaching. A digital version of the journal is available on the companion website.

Directions: Review the chapter cover page and the overview for this month. How do this month's topic, the quotes, phase, and affirmation relate to you right now? How are you feeling as you prepare for one year to end and to begin another? What do you feel confident about? Where do you need some help?

Use your journal to record your thoughts, feelings, and questions in a free-flowing narrative. This page is for your personal reflection; it does not need to be shared with your mentor unless you choose to do so. Now at the end of the year, you can review your monthly reflections to see how much you have grown.

If you are a 2+ year teacher, you are aware of the expectations for teaching in June. Your journal entry will delve deeper into your practice using the same questions.

June Entry Date_____

Today I feel . . .

_____

_____

_____

I am confident in the areas of . . .

_____

_____

_____

I need some help . . .

_____

_____

_____

JUNE

Questions for Participating in Mentoring Conversations

Sometimes you don't know what to ask your mentor because you don't know what you don't know! Review this list and choose some questions that are useful to you. How will your mentor respond? Will you schedule a face-to-face meeting, or a phone appointment, or send an e-mail? What works best for both of you? Reflect on your mentor's responses and think about what works for you. If you are a 2+ year teacher, these may not apply to you; however, there is always something new to learn.

Your Possible Questions

1. I need help in closing up my room. What should I do first?

2. How should I reflect on my year? Will you meet with me?

3. Should I seek feedback from others (students, parents, colleagues, etc.) to gain insights into my year?

4. Do you have any final words of advice as I complete my year?

Other questions I have. . .

Anticipate Your Mentor's Questions

1. What did you learn about yourself as a teacher this year?

2. What did you learn about your students and their families this year?

3. How can I help you complete the year and do your June closing work?

4. What can I do to assist you to prepare for next year?

JUNE

Meetings and Observations

Plan brief weekly meetings with your mentor. The ACTs in this chapter serve as mentoring conversation starters and can also be used to assess or review what you may already know about a given topic.

Plan to meet at times that allow you to have quality time together in a place without interruptions. Use this calendar to schedule your meetings and classroom visits to ensure they will happen! Include watching videos, reading pages in *The First Years Matter* as part of your *PLAN*. A digital version of this calendar (June Calendar.pdf) is available on the companion website.

Reflect on all the observations by your mentor. What was most effective? Did you like the short drop in visits, or did you prefer when your mentor watched you teach an entire lesson from start to finish? Ask your mentor if she would be willing to informally mentor you next year.

June Calendar

MONDAY	TUESDAY	WEDNESDAY	THURSDAY	FRIDAY

Use this calendar to PLAN the month with your mentor as well as to document meetings.

Companion
Website

JUNE

CONNECT to Additional Resources

CONNECT to School and District Resources

What resources exist in your school and community that could assist you in June?

CONNECT With Colleagues, Parents, and Families

Who in the school building may be able to help you with June needs?

How can parents be helpful in assisting you in reflecting on your first year?

CONNECT to Student Voices

What better way is there to know how well you succeeded this year than to ask your students? With the help of your mentor, create an end-of-the-year anonymous survey for all the students. Perhaps your mentor could administer the survey to ensure you get honest answers. Some possible questions could be (1) Which lesson or unit did you most enjoy this year? (2) How could I improve my teaching? (3) Was I fair to all students? Why do you say that? and (4) What advice do you have for me as I prepare for next year?

CONNECT to Education Hot Topics

Play in School! Some research is showing that free play helps the brain and motivates the learner to be more creative. Most schools are limiting recess and any playtime, but after tests are done at the end of the year, some teachers are finding that playtime is fun and it is engaging their students. Discuss ways you can integrate free play to continue to promote learning in June.

CONNECT With the Companion Website

Video links, forms for this chapter, a featured book, and other resources by the author are located at resources.corwin.com/mentoringinaction.

JUNE

The First ACT!

Differentiating Mentoring Conversations

Teaching is complex work, and you can easily become overwhelmed. It is appropriate to customize your mentoring conversations so that your mentor is responding to your needs and skills. If you are a 2+ year teacher, use this template as a self-reflection or share it in your novice teacher support group.

Directions: Discuss the prompts with your mentor or think about them on your own. Refer to your state or district teaching standards to note a common language for teaching and summarize your key ideas in each box. Skim the ACTs for this month and decide which topics are most relevant to your needs this month.

Name_____ Date _____

Monthly Needs Assessment

1. What is going well in your classroom right now?	3. What would you like to improve or enhance in your practice this month?
2. How do you know your practice is working? What is your evidence of success?	4. Review the ACT overview of possible conversations for this month with your mentor. What would you like to focus on this month?

A digital version of this template (Monthly Needs Assessment Sample With Standards.pdf) is available on the companion website. Keep a copy of this assessment in your professional file.

Companion Website

JUNE

Overview of the ACTs for June Conversations

Directions: Skim the ACTivities listed here and complete the pages that will forward your learning. If you are a 2+ year teacher, revisit any ACTs you already completed or try some new ACTs to stretch your thinking. Digital copies of some of the ACTs are available on the companion website.

Key Question Topic	ACTivities	PAGE
Reflect	ACT 1 **Letter to Yourself**	243
Reflect	ACT 2 **Novice Teacher Letter to Mentor**	244
Reflect	ACT 3 **Novice Teacher Letter to Future First-Year Teachers**	245
Closing	ACT 4 **Closing Procedures for the Classroom**	246
Closing	ACT 5 **Novice Teacher Letter to Students**	247
Students	ACT 6 **Classroom and Behavior Management Issues**	248
Communicate	ACT 7 **Communicating With Parents**	249
Communicate	ACT 8 **Sharing the Professional Portfolio**	250

JUNE

Letter to Yourself

Key Question: How do you culminate your year of teaching?

Directions: Write a letter to yourself highlighting your growth and acknowledging the work you have done with your mentor this year. Use the InTASC standards, the teacher evaluation categories, and the topics below as a guide for your letter.

> Personal growth
>
> Professional growth
>
> Social and emotional growth
>
> Teaching ability
>
> Interaction with my mentor
>
> Interaction with colleagues

Dear Self,

This year has been an exciting year full of surprises and challenges.

Select all or some of these stems to guide your thinking.

> I have learned . . .
>
> I feel good about . . .
>
> Personally, I appreciate the way I was able to . . .
>
> I see myself . . . next year.
>
> I really enjoyed . . .
>
> I am confident that . . .
>
> The best thing about being a beginning teacher is . . .
>
> I am looking forward to next year because . . .
>
> My mentor helped me . . .
>
> As a 2+ year teacher, I am continuing to learn . . .

It has been a great year for learning.

Sincerely,
YOU!

Novice Teacher Letter to Mentor

Key Question: How can you thank your mentor and culminate the experience?

Directions: Write your reflections of what you learned this year in a letter to your mentor. Use some of the prompts from ACT 1 to guide you. This is an opportunity for you to thank your mentor for all she has done for you. It is an important way to close the year and wind down the formal relationship you have had all year. Writing a letter is more effective than just telling your mentor what you appreciate because he can refer back to it at a later time.

Sample Letter Prompts

Dear Mentor,

I have learned . . .

I feel good about . . .

I appreciate the way you helped me . . .

I really enjoyed . . .

You helped me . . .

I am looking forward to next year because . . .

I see myself . . . next year.

I especially liked the way you . . .

I am confident that . . .

Companion
Website

Sincerely,
Your Mentee

JUNE

Novice Teacher Letter to Future First-Year Teachers

Key Question: How can you share what you have learned with other teachers?

Directions: Write an open letter to future teachers who will be hired to teach at your school next year. If you know novice teachers are being hired in the school next year, consider talking with them to help them transition more easily. Share the letter with your mentor and ask her to put it in the Survival packet or Welcome to our School binder. Put your name and room number on the letter and offer your help to any novice who would like to meet with you. Novice teachers next year will appreciate the advice from another beginner!

Date: _____

Dear First-Year Teacher,

I have just completed my first year, and I have some advice and suggestions for you as you begin preparing yourself for your first class.

Use these stems or create your own.

Some advice I have for you about planning is . . .

What I learned this year is . . .

I can help you with . . .

Ways you can expect your mentor to support you include . . .

What I most enjoyed this year is . . .

Welcome to our school!

Sincerely,

Your name and contact information

Grade Level

Closing Procedures for the Classroom

Key Question: How do you close out your classroom?

Directions: Meet with your mentor to discuss in detail how you should close the classroom and what must be handed in to the office the last day of school. Very often, teacher induction programs do a great job of orienting novice teachers to the school but forget about you at the end of the year. Be proactive and ask your mentor for help. There are cultural norms in schools for doing certain things certain ways. This doesn't mean you shouldn't question things and try to make them better; it just means you need to know what the school culture is and why it is that way. Often what happens is that novices don't know what is expected, and they are left doing everything alone the last day of school or after the students are dismissed. Make sure you know what is expected weeks ahead of time to avoid the stress of closing a classroom. Don't be that teacher alone on the last day of school.

1. **Possible paperwork might include**

   - Grades for students by a certain dates

   - Promotion cards

   - Paperwork for retaining students

   - Report cards for principal review a week before students get them

   - Special needs student reports and IEPs

   - Other . . .

2. **Closing the room may involve**
   - Covering all the shelves with paper
   - Removing all the books
   - Putting materials in storage
   - Washing and cleaning desks
   - Putting away technology
   - Other . . .

Novice Teacher Letter to Students

Key Question: How can you culminate the year with your students?

Directions: One way to close out the year is to write a class letter to the students. It provides closure to the year, and it lets the students know you care about them. Ask your mentor to read your letter before you send it out. It does not have to be long, but it should contain specific highlights from the year and be authentic. Use this sample to guide your conversation.

Sample Letter to Students

Dear Class,

It has been a great year. I would like to highlight some key memories for me as your teacher.

List some specific memories of positive days in class.

I am grateful for . . .

You have been an outstanding class . . .

Thank you for . . .

You taught me a lot about teaching . . . like . . .

I learned from you too . . . for example . . .

I look forward to seeing you . . .

Sincerely,
Your Teacher

Classroom and Behavior Management Issues

Key Question: How do I close out the year successfully?

Directions: The year is coming to a close. One last month, and it could be the most difficult. You may not know what to expect, and students are anxious to get out of school. This is the time when some disruptive behavior can emerge. When high-stakes tests are done, students tend to think the year is over. This is the time to review all the ACTs at the end of the months that relate to Classroom and Behavior Management. Ask your mentor for advice about minimizing off task behavior at the end of the year.

Which ACTs do you need to revisit at this time?

Month	ACT	Key Question
September	ACT 8	How do routines minimize disruption and promote a positive learning environment?
October	ACT 8	What do you need to think about before disciplining a student?
November	ACT 8	How can you learn how to minimize misbehavior?
December	ACT 8	How do you learn how to manage degrees of inappropriate behavior?
January	ACT 8	How can you brainstorm solutions to your common problems?
February	ACT 6	What are appropriate rewards for students?
March	ACT 6	How can you document student meetings?
April	ACT 6	How can you document changes in student behavior?
May	ACT 6	What do you need to know at the end of the year?

Companion Website

Communicating With Parents

Key Question: What do you need to communicate to parents at the end of the year?

Directions: Write a letter or year-end report to all parents of the students in your class. The purpose is to thank them for supporting their children to be successful and to let them know what you thought about this group of students.

The end of the year is a hectic and incredibly exhausting time for any teacher. Novice teachers are especially overwhelmed because they have never closed a year before. You may have to hold a student back or give a report card that is less than satisfactory. Parents may or may not have been as cooperative as you may have liked, and as a teacher, you have to look at the big picture. In spite of any challenges, this is a time to celebrate the completion of a year and acknowledge what you have done successfully.

The final report cards will focus on the academic work, which is very important. However, there is an opportunity for you to use this final communication to stay connected to the parents. There may be siblings coming through the system, and it is nice for you to know the family ahead of time. Just as in the beginning of the year you wrote a letter of introduction, it is important at the end of the year to write some kind of closing note to parents. This is the novice teacher's first year of teaching, and it is important to take the time to reflect on what went well and to share that with parents and students. You may consider combining the student letter in ACT 5 and the parent letter.

Brainstorm ways with your mentor that this could be a doable and enjoyable task. You may also consider a closing of the year website or to send an e-mail with class photos and direct the parents there. The goal is to end on a positive note with parents!

Ask your mentor for ideas:

JUNE

Sharing the Professional Portfolio

Key Question: How do you culminate the year sharing your successes?

Directions: If you created a portfolio (see Part I Figure 9 and ACT 2 May) this is the time to share it! Collaborate with your mentor and other novice teachers to host a portfolio sharing party. Bring food, play music, and place the portfolios on a table where guests can flip though and sign the register. The guest register page will allow attendees to sign in and make a brief comment that you can read later.

Consider videotaping yourself with your portfolio. Just talk about a page or two and share what you learned by completing this portfolio. Think about sharing your portfolio next year with the incoming first-year teachers in August when they begin the school year.

Invite:

- other beginning teachers
- your principal or department chair
- parents
- community or business partners you developed this year

Share your portfolio with your mentor first as a practice session. Celebrate!

Companion
Website

June Novice Teacher Reflections

Directions: Complete any of these prompts to summarize your experience this month, or add your own. Compare and share your reflections with your mentor or other novice teachers in your support group. You can also reflect on these prompts in your Novice Teacher Journal.

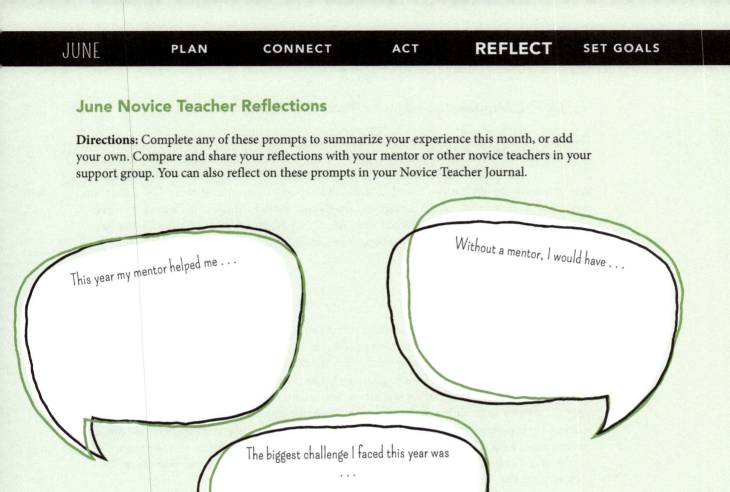

This year my mentor helped me . . .

Without a mentor, I would have . . .

The biggest challenge I faced this year was . . .

As a 2+ year teacher, I learned . . .

What I look forward to most next year is . . .

Using Mindfulness to Explore Teaching Dilemmas

Teaching is complex, and often there are not clear answers to situations that arise while you are being mentored. The teaching dilemmas introduced at the end of each month in the REFLECT section may not always apply to you; however, the process of reflecting on this dilemma will help you think about what you might do if this did happen to you. Sometimes when a situation arises that we didn't anticipate, we react and say things before we think. This journal process will allow you to pause and think about what you would like to say next. These dilemmas are useful for mentoring conversation starters, novice teacher support group discussions, and personal reflection.

Dilemma 11: Do You Ask to Be Mentored Again?

You have been mentored all year. You loved your mentor, and you met lots of novice teachers, and you really enjoyed it. You had so many questions, and your mentor helped you in many ways, but there is so much more to learn that you didn't have time to talk about. You heard that the district is writing a comprehensive plan to support novice teachers beyond their first year of teaching, and they are asking for volunteers. You are tired. It is the end of the year, and you just can't wait for summer break. It has been a wonderful year in many ways because you have successfully completed the year and are rehired! All of the time and energy spent on mentoring conversations have paid off. Your mentor has influenced your teaching, and you feel more confident and competent. However, continuing with your mentor for another year seems like a great opportunity. *What do you do?*

Respond to these prompts in your Novice Teacher Journal, available on the companion website.

1. State the dilemma as clearly as possible in one sentence if you can.

2. What decision do you need to make in regard to this situation?

3. Write about the emotions that come up for you that relate to this situation. If you have two choices, write how the emotions might be different.

4. Stop and reread what you have written. Underline any key words or phrases that stand out for you.

5. Soften your eyes or close them and take three deep breaths. Ask yourself, what am I missing that I have not noticed. Write that down in your journal.

6. How can your mentor help you? Write your reflection in your journal.

7. If you are truly stuck, bring your dilemma to another novice teacher, one in her or his second or third year of teaching. Ask him or her to listen and to ask you questions to clarify your dilemma. Ask her not to give advice, just to ask you questions to help you clarify your feelings and next steps.

8. How do you feel about this dilemma now? All dilemmas are not resolved! This is a process of clarifying and understanding how you feel and how you might proceed in the future.

Directions: Complete the goal-setting processes alone or with your mentor. Write your responses on this page or in your Novice Teacher Journal, available on the companion website. If you are a 2+ year teacher, reflect on how you are growing from year to year.

1. *Goal for Improving Your Teaching Practices*

   - Review the PLAN–CONNECT–ACT–REFLECT pages you completed in this chapter with your mentor. Look ahead to January ACTs to see what you may focus on to continue your development.

   - Acknowledge all you have done this year!

2. *Goal to Support Your Social and Emotional Well-Being*

   - Discuss any challenges you may be facing right now. Ask your mentor for help.
   - Search for books, articles, videos, and music that you enjoy and bring you a feeling of restful mindfulness. Include the activities that feel "right" to you in your daily life.
   - Goal:

> "My mentor helped me to become an effective teacher. I could not have navigated my first year without her.

—FIRST YEAR TEACHER

NOVICE TEACHER PHASE: SUCCESS!

"I am committed to learning how to teach. I can see the impact of my reflections and conversations with my mentor in my classroom. My students are successful!"

NOVICE TEACHER AFFIRMATION

I will reflect on my experience and acknowledge what I did well.

JULY

FINAL REFLECTION AND PLANNING FOR NEXT YEAR

Retreat, Reflect, Renew

GUIDING QUESTIONS

1. What have I learned that will improve my teaching practices?
2. What are the leadership opportunities for novice teachers in my district or school?

Interstate Teacher Assessment and Support Consortium—InTASC Standards

Review InTASC Standard 10.

- **Standard 10 Leadership and Collaboration**

The teacher seeks appropriate leadership roles and opportunities to take responsibility for student learning, to collaborate with learners, families, colleagues, other school professionals, and community members to ensure learner growth, and to advance the profession.

Chapter Overview

The year has ended. You have successfully completed your year of teaching. If this was your very first year you have learned so much! If this was your second or third year, you have learned more strategies for improving your teaching practices. This month-by-month curriculum was designed to support you, and the Novice Teacher Journal is a place where you can look back and see notes and ideas that you can use next year. You have done all the work all year long. This month is all about YOU. This is your time to think about what you learned, what you would do differently, and how you can participate as a novice teacher leader in your district.

A video of a retreat in ACT 2 will show you how mentors can rejuvenate in the summer and prepare for meeting their next group of mentees. Think about organizing a retreat in your district for novice teachers! Teachers finishing their first year and teachers in years 2+ know what will be useful to them. It would be useful and exciting to have teachers in their first five years of teaching come together in July or early August to share ideas and prepare for the opening of school. Ask your mentor or other experienced teachers to help you organize this and step up and take on a leadership role.

JULY

How can you help your district sustain a mentoring program for novice teachers? Ask your mentor how you can be part of the committee. Often district committees include only mentors and experienced teachers, but novice teachers have so many good ideas. If you district doesn't have a formal plan, ask to be part of the design team. Make sure your program includes mentoring for 2+ year teachers. You still need help and support after year one!

1. **Professional Development for Mentors**

   - Was your mentor prepared to mentor you?

   - How can you ensure mentors are trained to work with novice teachers?

2. **A District Action Plan**

   If your district does not have a plan for mentoring, consider being part of the design team.

   - Go to the MentoringinAction.com website to see the Interactive Guide for creating a District Action Plan.
   - Review plans from other districts.
   - Watch the videos that highlight key components of the plans.
   - Work with the experienced teachers to develop a plan that meets novice teacher needs.

JULY

CONNECT to Other Novice Teachers and Your Mentor

CONNECT to School and District Resources

What resources did you use this year? Do you need more resources next year?

CONNECT With Other Mentors, District Administrators, and Lead Mentors

By having monthly meetings with a mentor and a summer retreat for novice teachers, you can stay connected to other professionals and support each other. District Administrators need to develop a district plan with mentors and include novice teacher voices. Consider being part of that discussion.

CONNECT to Student Voices

Student voices and perspectives are integrated throughout this book because without student engagement, a teacher cannot be effective. Review all the ideas that relate to student voices and highlight the ones that you found most useful. The interactive PDF "Using Student Perspectives" has all of the videos and surveys in one place for easy access. Using this document at a novice teacher summer retreat or meeting can provide focus and keep students at the heart of teaching. Watching videos at meetings is engaging and brings a fresh perspective to the discussion.

CONNECT to Education Hot Topics

Review the Hot Topics and consider using them in professional development workshops with your mentors and other novice teachers at the school. They make great conversation starters and what would you do if . . . stems to develop mentor skills.

CONNECT With the Companion Website

Review all of the resources you have available to you and use them in your district professional development programs. A Video Library with many of the videos mentioned in this book is available on MentoringinAction.com. Click on novice teacher to see the videos that most apply to you. Each video in the library has a description and a reflective prompt, so it can easily be used in professional development meetings with mentors or novice teachers.

JULY

Companion Website

What Have You Learned?

Ask yourself . . .

- Would I be mentored again next year if the district offered this option to me? Why or why not?

- How would I use this book, *The First Years Matter,* and the Novice Teacher Journal next year in a continued mentoring experience?

- What is the most significant thing I learned this year with my mentor?

- What am I most grateful for in this mentoring process?

- As a 2+ year teacher using the book for the first time, I . . .

- As a 2+ year teacher using the book for the second time, I learned . . .

Retreat With Other Novice Teachers

Ask your district to sponsor a full day retreat in July or August where you can reflect and share ideas with other novice teachers. Watch the video titled *Mindful Mentoring Retreat* to hear how mentors took a day and valued their time together. In this video, the mentors are called Effective Educator Coaches. How could you use this event as a model for your day long retreat? How could your mentor help you organize this?

VIDEO 2.22

Mindful
Mentoring
Retreat

Sample Agenda

1. Welcome and Overview—District Leaders and Mentors

2. Sharing Best Teaching Practices—Novice Teacher Sharing

3. Solving Challenges Together—Small Group Sharing

4. Mindful Teaching—Promoting Health and Wellness in Mentors and Novice Teachers

5. Sharing Effective Practices for Opening the School Year

6. Journey Into Leadership Maps—A Creative Process (see teachers share in video)

7. Closing—Circle of Trust (watch *Mindful Mentoring Retreat* video)

JULY

Companion
Website

July Novice Teacher Reflections

- Review all of your Novice Teacher Journal entries and end-of-month chapter reflections. Look for themes and patterns in your writing.
- Respond to these prompts to summarize your thoughts.

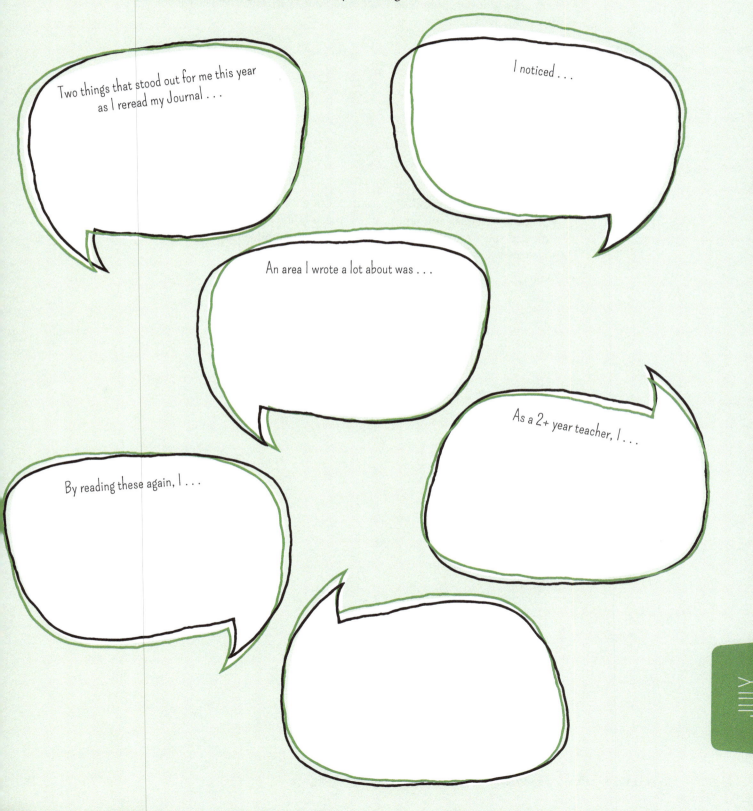

Two things that stood out for me this year as I reread my Journal . . .

I noticed . . .

An area I wrote a lot about was . . .

By reading these again, I . . .

As a 2+ year teacher, I . . .

Directions: Complete the goal-setting processes alone or with your mentor. Write your responses on this page or in your Novice Teacher Journal available on the companion website.

1. *Goal for Improving Your Teaching Practices*

   - Reflect on your teaching year. What stood out as effective? What will you do differently next year?

   - Goal:

2. *Goal to Support Your Social and Emotional Well-Being*

   - What were your biggest challenges this year? How did you handle them?

   - Continue to explore mindfulness and consider taking a retreat day for yourself. Use your senses to relax and renew. What makes you feel relaxed? How can you find the time and space to enjoy nature and the beauty around you? How can you create a space for yourself that allows you to renew?

   - Goal:

JULY

INDEX

CORWIN

A SAGE Publishing Company

CORWIN HAS ONE MISSION: to enhance education through intentional professional learning.

We build long-term relationships with our authors, educators, clients, and associations who partner with us to develop and continuously improve the best evidence-based practices that establish and support lifelong learning.

Solutions you want. Experts you trust. Results you need.